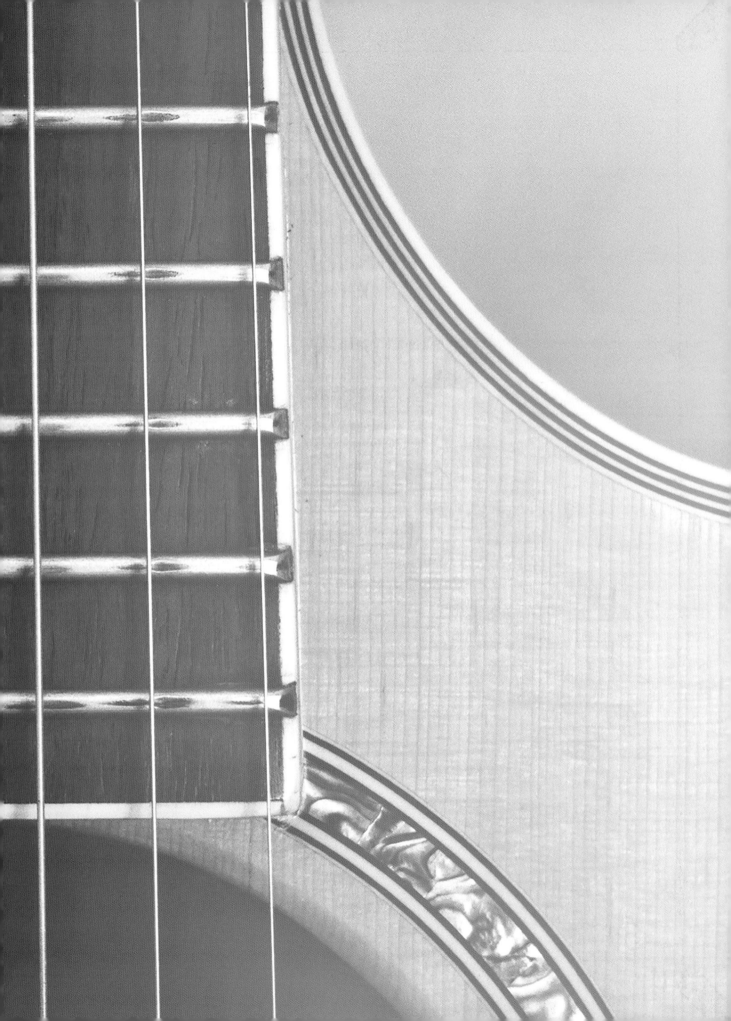

The Complete
Beginner's Guide to
Guitar

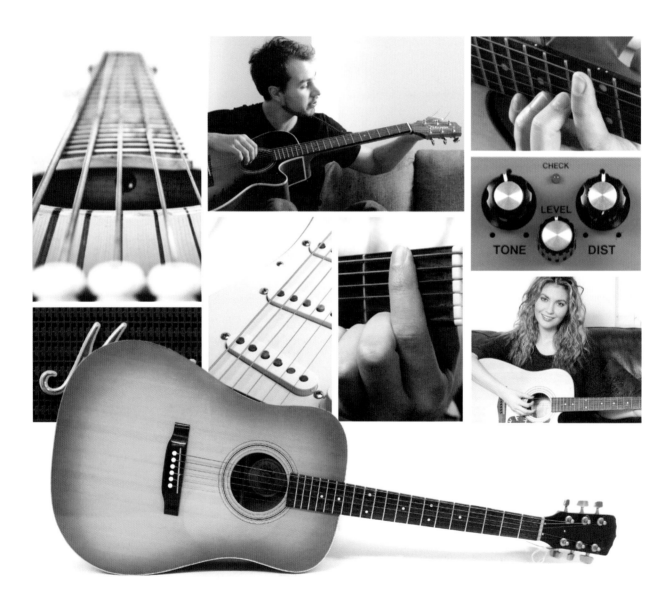

sona
BOOKS

sona
BOOKS

First published in the UK 2019 by Sona Books
an imprint of Danann Media Publishing Limited.

CAT NO: SON0436

ISBN: 978-1-912918-03-4

Made in EU.

Contents

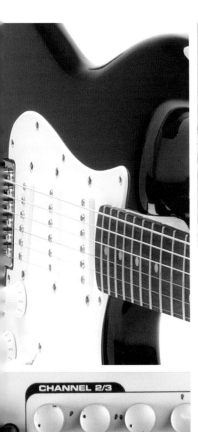

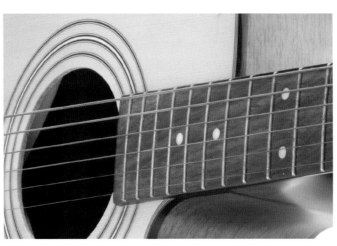

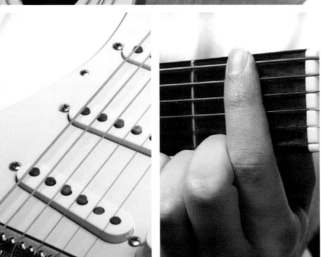

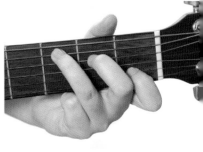

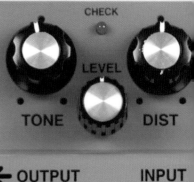

" *There are various types of guitar to consider in determining the sound you want to achieve*"

Getting started

The ultimate guide and step-by-step tutorials will teach you the basics, from choosing the right guitar and knowing how to hold it, to strumming and picking

The ultimate guide to the guitar

From picking up a guitar and strumming simple songs to playing jaw-dropping solos on stage, everyone's musical journey starts somewhere

So you've decided to make the leap and learn the guitar — that's great news. The benefits of playing really are plentiful, from simply helping you to relax to actually writing your own songs, performing live in front of a crowd and forging a professional career as a guitarist. So whatever your reason for starting to learn the guitar, once you have mastered all of the basics, you will be able to hear the results for yourself and slowly develop your own individual playing style.

There is far more to playing than simply picking up the instrument and blindly strumming the strings, though. As this feature will teach you, there are the various types of guitar to consider in determining the sound you want to achieve, eg do you learn on an acoustic or go straight for an electric? You will also need to learn chords — the correct strings to hold down in order to produce certain notes needed to play along to songs or write your own music — and tabs to play the riffs that inspired you to pick up a guitar in the first

Strings and frets

Throughout this bookazine, the horizontal lines on these tab diagrams (right) refer to the string you're fretting. The numbers refer to which fret you're playing (below).

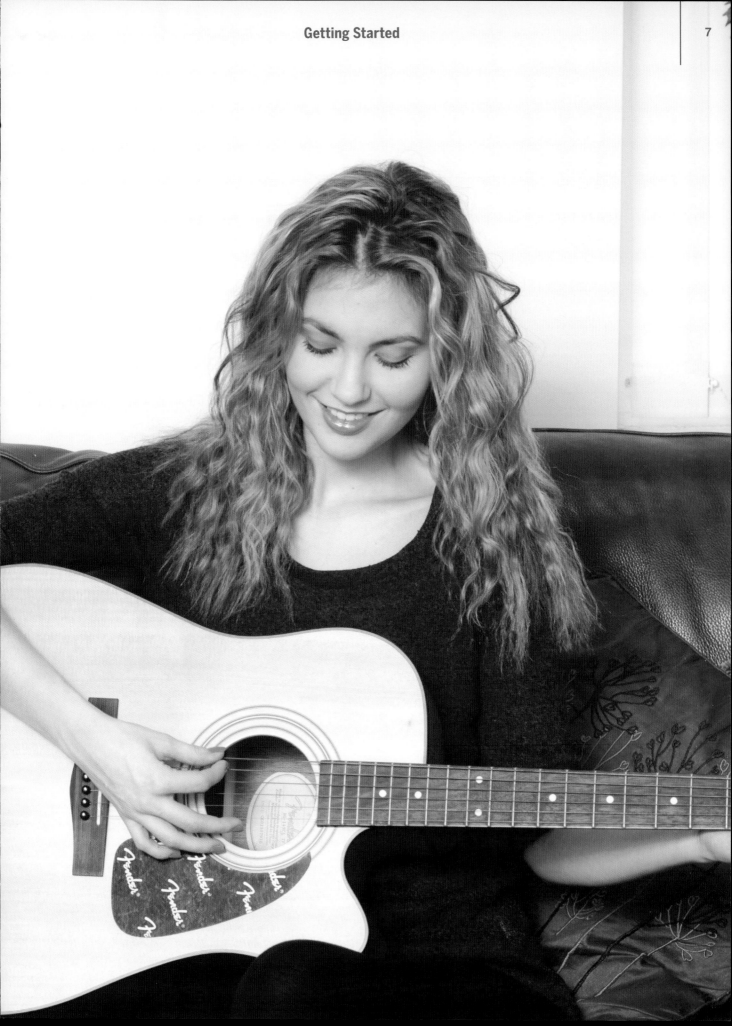

Anatomy of a guitar

Get to know your instrument inside and out, and discover all of the components

When learning to play the guitar, it is important to know what each part of the instrument is called and what its purpose is. You will find all of the parts listed here on an acoustic guitar and its variants. Most of the parts also present on electric guitars.

Hollow body

The body of an acoustic guitar is large and hollow, acting as a resonating chamber that amplifies the strings. In the body is a sound hole, situated underneath the strings, which is how the sound enters the hollow body when you play

Saddle and bridge

The bridge of the guitar is the piece of material by which the bottom of the strings are attached to the guitar. The saddle is the small strip on top of the bridge and its grooves help separate the strings and hold them into position

Pick guard

The flat, smooth piece of material placed near the sound hole on most guitars, including electric models, is called the pick guard. This helps to protect that area of the guitar from scratches when your hand travels as you strum, in case you touch the body

Sound hole

The sound hole is the part of the guitar that helps project the sound, and is found on all types of guitar except for electric. When playing, strumming the strings over the sound hole helps to generate volume

Dots

Some guitars have dots placed within some of the frets along the fretboard. These are reference points that are always on the fifth, seventh, ninth and twelfth frets to help you get your fingers into the correct positions

place. Most importantly, you will discover the need to practise and not get disheartened if you don't progress as quickly as you might like. This is the hurdle that many newcomers fail to overcome, but by giving up before you have really started you will be depriving yourself of one of the most satisfying skills you could ever hope to learn. So make sure you stick with it and read on to find out more about this amazing instrument.

Buying your guitar

When purchasing your first guitar, you need to ask yourself what type of music you want to play to ascertain the best type of guitar to buy. There are four main types — classical, acoustic, acoustic-electric/electro-acoustic and electric. Classical guitars are acoustic-based but are strung with nylon strings and have large fretboards, making them perfect for beginners working on their chord formations. Acoustic guitars are very similar in appearance, but the strings are traditionally steel and the necks are thinner, making them ideal for smaller hands. Acoustic-electric guitars come with a built-in pickup and can be connected to amps to boost the volume, electric guitars feature thin necks and rely on amps to produce the sound.

When in the market for a guitar, check out your local music stores and make a point of trying out a range of models to find the shape and feel that appeals to you. Try to play as many guitars as time allows to help you gauge the different sounds they make, and work out your budget early so that you can focus on guitars that suit your price range. Even if you are planning on buying online, it is important to have some hands-on experience with the type of guitar you want so that when it arrives you'll know if it sounds as it should do.

> *"When purchasing your first guitar, you need to ask yourself what type of music you want to play to ascertain the best type of guitar to buy"*

Getting started

When you are taking your first tentative steps into the world of guitar playing, it is important to do things by the book. The reason for this is so that you don't develop bad habits that can hinder your progress and playing technique further down the line. Sure, when you master the basics and start to explore your preferred playing style, you can adopt whatever rock 'n' roll posture you like, but when just starting out it will really help you to ensure you are seated correctly, with good posture and your hands in the right positions.

As well as providing advice on how to sit or stand correctly while playing your guitar, this book touches on a number of other basics to help you lay solid foundations for future learning. We describe how best to hold your pick, how to limber up with simple warm up exercises and guide you through strumming your first notes. So make sure you concentrate on nailing these initial principles before progressing any further.

There is no right or wrong way to learn guitar and there are certainly many pros and cons for teaching yourself versus

Neck and nut
From the headstock, the strings of the guitar are guided along the neck by the nut, a piece of material made out of plastic or bone into which small grooves are cut. You will put your fingers on various parts of the neck to create different notes

Fretboard and frets
Dotted along the neck of the guitar are frets. These refer to the metal strips that separate the neck into sections, but frets are generally referred to by guitarists as the space in between the metal strips where you hold the strings to alter the pitch

Headstock and tuners
The headstock is the top of the guitar and is attached to the neck. On the headstock are tuners, which you will use to adjust the pitch of each of the strings on the guitar and tune it up. You use the machine heads to turn the pegs

paying a professional tutor to guide you. Some say that the sense of accomplishment is heightened if you use books or DVDs to help you and, indeed, some of music's greatest players are self-taught (or so they claim). If you are serious about playing, we would recommend taking a few lessons just to ensure that your playing posture (as well as other considerations) is correct going forward. Other than that, so as long as you set aside half an hour to an hour a day for practice, you'll soon be reaping the rewards.

Types of guitar playing

When you first start learning guitar you will probably have some idea of the type of player you would like to eventually become. It may be that you just fancy strumming simple songs around the campfire, in which case all you will need to know are some basic chords and a good strumming technique. If you want to play rock or metal music, an electric guitar is a must and you'll need to train your fretting hand to craft power and barre chords, as well as develop a good technique for picking strings using a plectrum. If your future lies in lead guitar, you'll need to practise all kinds of scales to play solos, master the art of alternate picking (a plectrum technique that involves alternating your upward and downward strokes to play faster) and learn to be able to improvise your own solos. Some people assume that rhythm guitarists are in some way inferior to lead guitarists, but often the opposite is true. To be a rhythm guitarist you must have mastered a wide range of chords and be able to switch seamlessly between them while maintaining a constant strumming rhythm, arpeggios, chord riffs, chord solos and complex strums. A rhythm guitarist is the constant driving force behind a song and is equally as important as the percussion section in maintaining the flow and pace of the song, whereas the lead guitarist plays over the top and embellishes certain sections to give the song more vibrancy and a clear hook.

Musicality

While it is by no means essential to be able to read music to learn the guitar, it will provide a good grounding for you to develop as a player and allow you to borrow arrangements from other types of music, such as piano. Probably the most essential skill to develop as a player, though, is a sense of rhythm in your strumming. It's all very well being able to strum your strings in a down and up motion,

but being able to keep time doing it and develop strumming patterns is key to building your own style and stamping your own mark on the songs you are going to play.

If you would like to improve your fingering on the frets in terms of speed and accuracy, then scales (a series of consecutive notes played in succession) are part of the learning process that will put you in good stead for licks and solos. And learning scales is extremely useful, even if you never play a solo in your entire life. By just playing chords you will never break out of the ordinary, so you need to connect your chords with scales. If you want to play particular songs on your guitar, rather than strumming chords (which

Hollow body
The body of an acoustic guitar is large and hollow, acting as a resonating chamber that amplifies the strings. In the body is a sound hole, situated underneath the strings, which is how the sound enters the hollow body when you play

Strings types
Classical acoustic guitars use nylon strings, which are easy on the hands and ideal for . Steel-string acoustic guitars feature steel strings that will cause more discomfort on the fingers when starting out, but create a much crisper sound

> *"To be a rhythm guitarist you must have mastered a wide range of chords"*

Acoustic guitars

Acoustic guitars require no additional amplification equipment and are ideal for beginners learning the basics

Acoustic guitars come in two main forms: classical and steel-string. Classical guitars have a wider neck and use nylon strings, making them perfect for beginners. This is because the nylon strings are easy on the fingers — both in terms of fretting and strumming — and the wide necks give your fretting hand a thorough workout, making you stretch further to form the chords. The benefit of this is that once you have learned to form the chords on a classical guitar, everything else is a piece of cake! Steel strings produce a defined and sharp sound that is a distinctive component of a wide range of popular music styles — from rock to country — but they can feel harsh on the fingers at first.

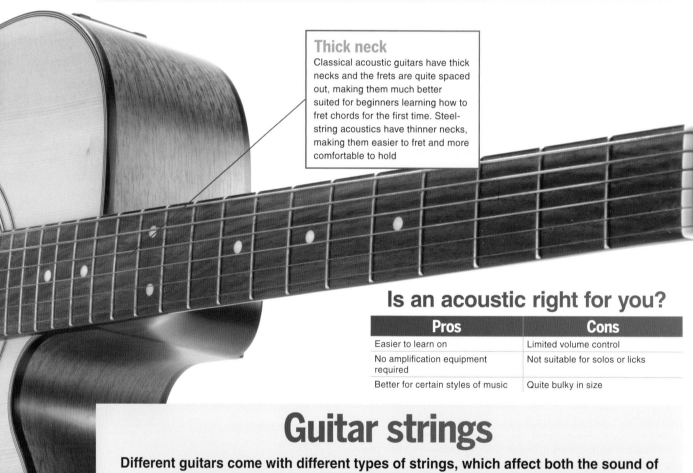

Thick neck
Classical acoustic guitars have thick necks and the frets are quite spaced out, making them much better suited for beginners learning how to fret chords for the first time. Steel-string acoustics have thinner necks, making them easier to fret and more comfortable to hold

Is an acoustic right for you?

Pros	Cons
Easier to learn on	Limited volume control
No amplification equipment required	Not suitable for solos or licks
Better for certain styles of music	Quite bulky in size

Guitar strings

Different guitars come with different types of strings, which affect both the sound of the instrument and the ease of playing. We examine the various types

The sound that your guitar makes depends a lot on the type of strings used and their gauge (thickness). The higher the gauge, the thicker the string and, likewise, the lower the gauge, the thinner the string. Higher gauged strings will generally last longer and provide a much meatier, fatter sound, whereas thinner strings generate a lighter, crisper sound.

Nylon strings, like those found on classical acoustic guitars are smoother, more comfortable to press down and easier to slide your fingers along, making them ideal for beginners. Acoustic and electric guitars commonly use steel strings, which produce the fullest sound but are harder on the fingers and will inevitably cause a degree of discomfort on your fretting hand. You can get around this problem by switching to lower-gauged strings, which are thinner and easier to press down on, or by practising so that you become accustomed to the initial discomfort and the skin on your fingers grows a little harder and becomes calloused.

are the basic foundations of any song), then you can use tabs. Tabs are a form of musical notation that tell the player where to put their fingers on the guitar neck and once you've learnt how to read them you'll be playing your way through all of the Fender-bending classics in a matter of days.

Playing with others

We've said it already, but we really can't stress enough the importance of practise in your development as a player. Even if you think that you have learnt something, if you don't practise it for days after, by the time you go back you will have forgotten at least part of it. So keep momentum with your playing and try to practise for at least half an hour every day to keep your mind and muscles well trained. Dedication to your instrument will have you strumming from muscle memory in no time.

Of course, the reason why you got into guitar in the first place could be because you want to form or join a band, in which case practising with others is a great way to develop all aspects of your playing, from simple timing and coordination through to improvisation. With a dedicated rhythm section keeping the beat, it is much easier to perfect a smoother, more natural style than if you are sat alone in your attic room. And there is nothing like a room full of musicians, whatever the level of expertise, to inspire each other and bounce ideas around — which takes us back to the argument over whether it is best to learn from books and DVDs or a professional tutor. While the aforementioned formats will get you so far, nothing beats the advice or tutorage of a fellow player, so take the time to explore the scene in your area and see if any local bands rent nearby practice space so you can drop in. Try to attend as many gigs and live shows as you can, too, because just watching other guitarists perform can help you pick up useful tips on how to play your instrument.

> *"If you would like to improve your fingering, then scales are part of the process"*

Hard body

Unlike the bodies of acoustic guitars, which have hollow bodies to amplify the sound, electric guitars have hard bodies, which are much thinner and easier to hold. Situated on the body are dials to adjust the sound coming out of the instrument

Toggle switch

The switch on the front of electric guitars is used to toggle between pickups to produce different sounds. For example, the up position engages the pickup closest to the neck to produce a mellower sound, the middle position engages the top and middle pickups and the down position engages just the pickup closest to the bridge

Electric guitars

**The electric guitar is the workhorse of popular music
from rock, blues and jazz to pop — and can create very distinct styles**

Unlike acoustic guitars, which are usually self-amplifying, electric guitars need to be plugged into a stand-alone amplifier to be heard adequately. Acoustic-electric guitars are the exception as they can be plugged in and amplified as well. They are usually solid-body guitars (although archtop electric guitars are available that have hollow bodies to give them more acoustic resonance) with pickups situated beneath the strings where you strum that channel the sound through the amp. The pickups and amplifier used with a solid-body electric guitar create a metallic sound with a lengthy sustain, and the design variations among electric guitars allows them to produce a wide variety of tones. The two most popular designs, the Fender Stratocaster and the Gibson Les Paul, have their own distinct sound and, as such, you'll soon be able to tell which guitar features in different songs.

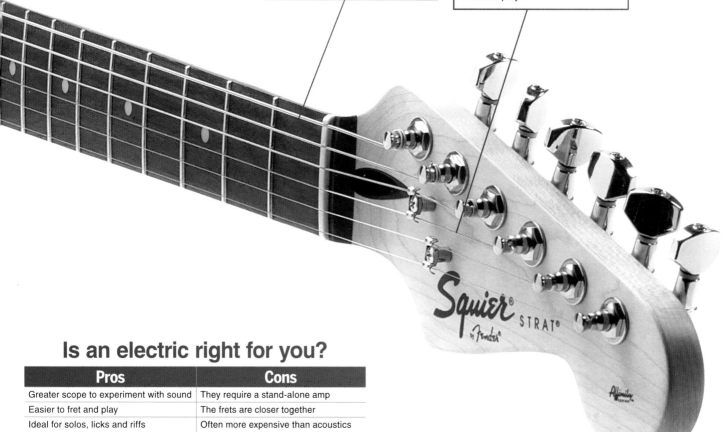

Pickups

Situated on the body of all electric guitars, underneath the strings where you strum, are three rows of pickups. These transducer devices capture the vibrations of the strings as you play them and convert them into an electrical signal that is then broadcast through the amp

Small frets

As the necks of electric guitars are much thinner than those of acoustics, fretting the strings is much easier and you can also employ some techniques more easily than you can on an acoustic, such as fret-tapping and string-bending

Thin strings

The strings of an electric guitar are thinner than those used on acoustic guitars and they sit closer to the neck, making them easier to hold down. This doesn't necessarily make them easier to learn on, but once you have mastered the art of fretting on an electric, anything else is child's play!

Is an electric right for you?

Pros	Cons
Greater scope to experiment with sound	They require a stand-alone amp
Easier to fret and play	The frets are closer together
Ideal for solos, licks and riffs	Often more expensive than acoustics

How a guitar makes noise

The more you know about how the guitar makes the sound it does, the more effective a player you'll become

As we have already explored, acoustic guitars have large, hollow bodies into which the sound is channelled via a sound hole that sits under the strings. Most acoustic guitars also have a waist, or a narrowing, which makes it easier to rest the instrument on your knee and reach your arm around while playing.

Above and below the waist are widenings, known as bouts. The upper bout is where the neck connects and the lower bout is where the bridge is attached. The size and shape of the body and the bouts has a lot to do with the tone that a given guitar produces. When your choosing your first guitar, keep an ear out for these different tones.

When you hold down the strings of a guitar and strum them, the strings vibrate and transmit their vibrations to the saddle, the saddle then transmits these to the soundboard (the front of the guitar) and the soundboard and body amplify the notes. This is what then comes out of the sound hole.

Create a guitar sound
Try this simple method to get the right technique

01 Strum the guitar
Place your guitar on your knee, place your strumming hand over the sound hole and strum the open strings.

02 Change positions
Now move your strumming hand further down the base of the guitar towards the bridge and again strum the strings. Hear the difference?

03 Press on the strings
Now experiment by holding down different strings, using your fretting hand on the neck, and notice the change in pitch when playing above or below the sound hole.

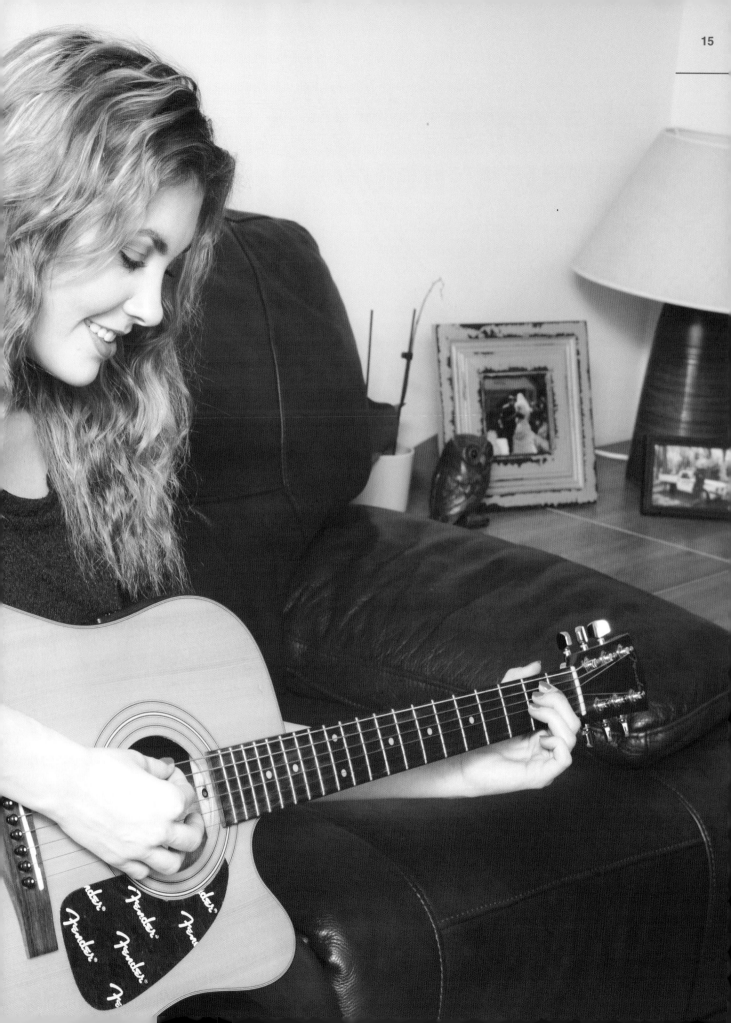

Take care of your guitar

If you want your instrument to continue producing crisp, defined sounds, you need to take good care of it

You should treat your guitar with the utmost respect, not only to keep it looking beautiful, but to make sure that you get the best possible sound out of your instrument. Things like dust can muffle the notes, so it is worth cleaning regularly and storing your guitar somewhere sensible. If you neglect your instrument, it could become damaged and not produce the results that you want. Here are some handy dos and don'ts when it comes to handling your guitar.

Clean your guitar
How best to go about cleaning the instrument

01 Loosen the strings
Start off by loosening the strings of your acoustic or electric guitar slightly. This only needs to be just enough to get a cloth under them and clean the vital components.

02 Clean around components
Using a dry cloth, wipe away the accumulated dust around the pickups of an electric guitar or around the bridge of an acoustic guitar. This area attracts a lot of dust if not maintained.

03 Things to avoid
Never spray your guitar with chemicals to clean it (as they might discolour it) and never use a wet cloth to clean steel strings as they will rust. If in doubt, buy new strings.

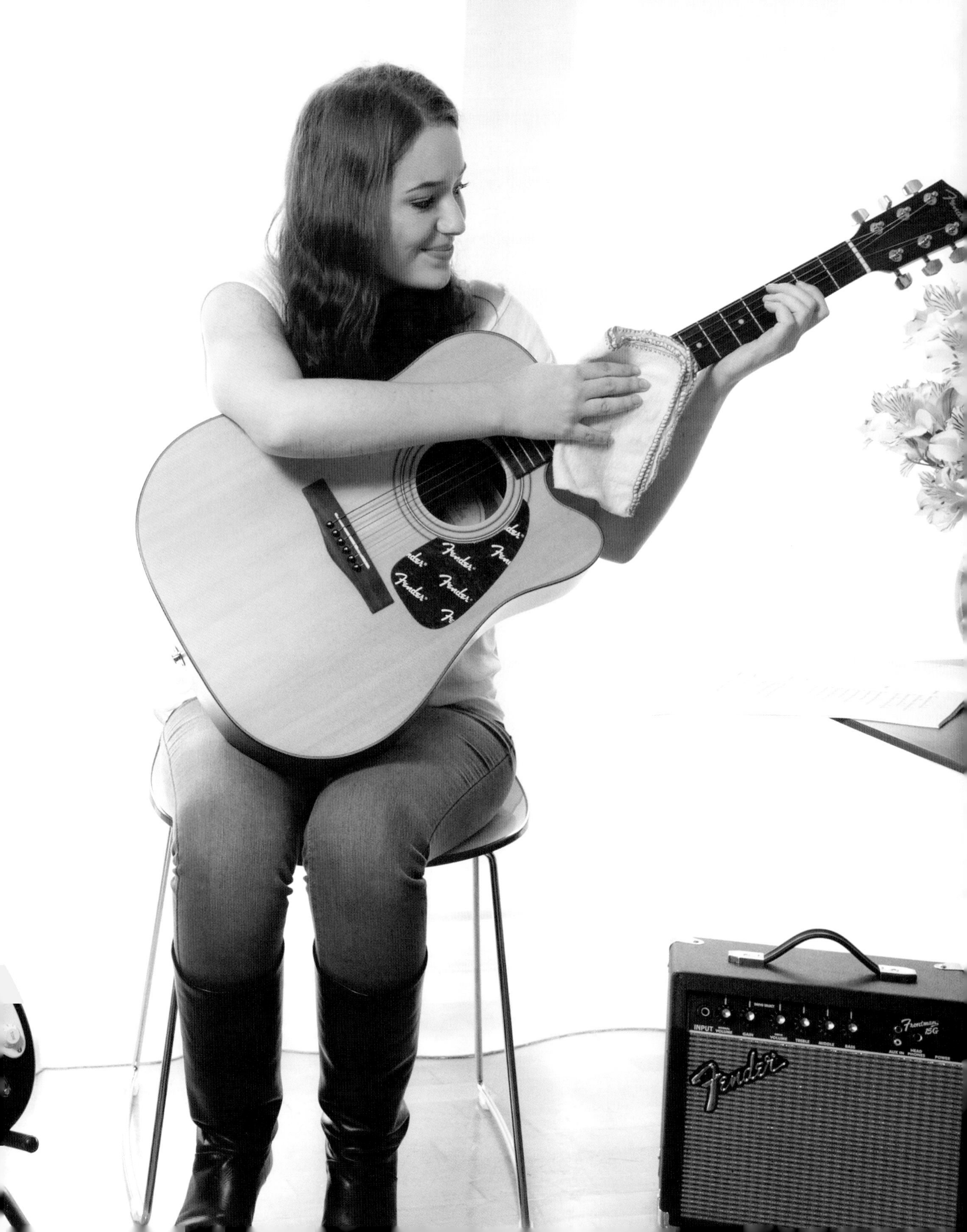
Fender
Frontman 15G
INPUT

Essential accessories

As with any hobby, there are a wide range of accessories available for guitar players to make playing easier. Here we take a look at some essential kit

From straps to tuners, slides to strings, there is almost no end of accessories that you can buy for your guitar. Some are essential for the transportation and well-being of your instrument, others simply enhance the cosmetics, change the sound

it makes or enable you to play in a particular way. Here we take you through the variety of add-ons available for you to purchase, and recommend some essentials and some of our favourite buys.

Slides

Slide guitar, or bottleneck, is a particular method for playing the guitar in which a slide is placed upon the string to vary its vibrating length and pitch. This slide can be moved along the string without lifting, creating continuous transitions in the pitch. Often made out of glass or metal, slides come in many styles.

Straps

If you want to play your guitar standing up, or you just want a little extra security while playing seated, a guitar strap is a must-have accessory. Adjustable straps come in a variety of styles and colours, and are easily put in place on your instrument by the attached pins.

Hard cases

If you perform gigs or generally transport your guitar around a lot, a hard case is well worth investing in. These cases snugly house your guitar and provide tough exterior protection so that your instrument won't get damaged, even if the case gets bashed around in transit.

Leads

If you play an electric guitar then you will need a cable in order to connect your instrument to your amp. The variety of these leads is staggering; not just in style and the materials used, but also the length. So if you are intending to play gigs and move around the stage you'll need something that won't restrict your strutting.

Strings

If you want your instrument to continue sounding great, then you will need to regularly restring it and keep plenty of additional strings handy if one breaks while you are playing — which they will do through regular use or if they become stretched. Strings vary in thickness, so experiment with the different gauges to get the sound you want.

Picks

Without growing the fingernails on your strumming hand, the easiest way to rhythmically strum your guitar is by using a plectrum — or pick. These little playing aids can be fashioned out of anything from plastic to glass, are shaped like an isosceles triangle with curved edges, and vary in width for different sounds and styles.

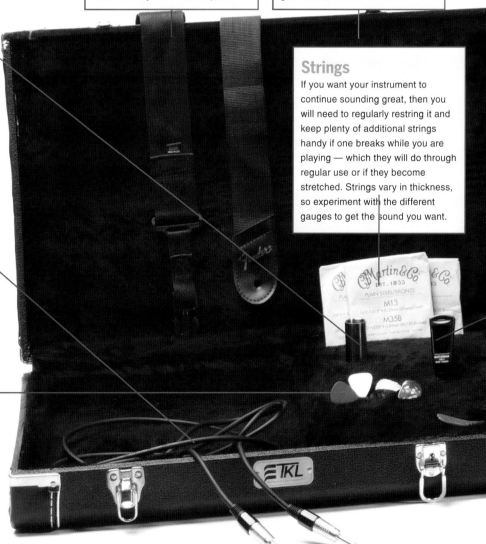

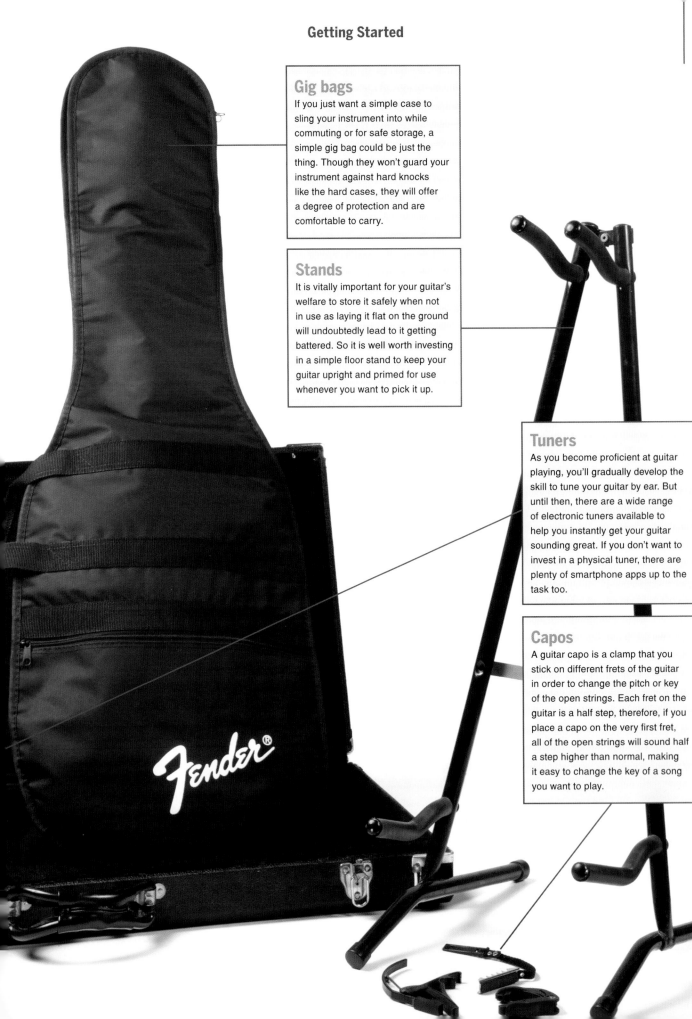

Gig bags

If you just want a simple case to sling your instrument into while commuting or for safe storage, a simple gig bag could be just the thing. Though they won't guard your instrument against hard knocks like the hard cases, they will offer a degree of protection and are comfortable to carry.

Stands

It is vitally important for your guitar's welfare to store it safely when not in use as laying it flat on the ground will undoubtedly lead to it getting battered. So it is well worth investing in a simple floor stand to keep your guitar upright and primed for use whenever you want to pick it up.

Tuners

As you become proficient at guitar playing, you'll gradually develop the skill to tune your guitar by ear. But until then, there are a wide range of electronic tuners available to help you instantly get your guitar sounding great. If you don't want to invest in a physical tuner, there are plenty of smartphone apps up to the task too.

Capos

A guitar capo is a clamp that you stick on different frets of the guitar in order to change the pitch or key of the open strings. Each fret on the guitar is a half step, therefore, if you place a capo on the very first fret, all of the open strings will sound half a step higher than normal, making it easy to change the key of a song you want to play.

Restring your guitar

Whether you've snapped a string or your guitar is sounding dull, restringing is essential and can give it a whole new lease of life

Restringing your guitar is an important part of any guitar owner's relatively small maintenance schedule, and while it might seem a little daunting when you do it for the first time, the whole restringing process is actually a lot easier than you might think.

How often you choose to restring your instrument really depends on a number of factors, such as how often you play, your playing style itself and the quality of strings on your instrument. Some guitarists will change their strings every week if they're gigging regularly, others may leave it far longer if they're only an occasional player. It's not an exact science, but there are a few clues that can help you decide it's time for a change; first of all, your strings will start to sound duller than when they were brand new, and secondly, they'll lose their shiny appearance. If you're noticing either or both of

these characteristics in your strings, then it's time to give your guitar a new lease of life.

As we've already mentioned, the first time you restring your guitar may seem like a daunting prospect, but it's far easier than you think, and once you get used to it, it'll take no time at all. It's always worth remembering that most good guitar shops will offer to restring your guitar for you for a small fee, so if you're not feeling particularly confident, there's help at hand there. That said, we're sure that by following the guide below, restringing your guitar should be easy.

> *"Restringing is an important part of any guitarist's maintenance schedule"*

Restringing Change your guitar's strings

01 Detune your guitar
Detune the string you wish to replace by turning the tuning peg. Make sure you turn it until the string is completely loose. To save time and energy, you can use a string winder.

02 Feed it through
If you're restringing an acoustic, remove the bridge pin and insert your new string into the bridge pin hole. If you're using an electric, feed the strings through the back of your guitar into the bridge.

A few things to watch out for as you restring

Finish the job

Finish the job Once you've fitted your new strings, it's time to tune up. It's worth noting you may need to do this a few times as you 'play in' the strings. It can take some practise so you may need a guide at first.

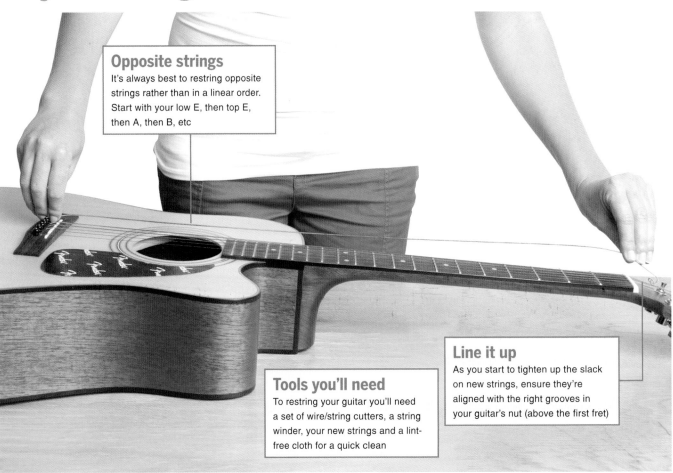

Opposite strings

It's always best to restring opposite strings rather than in a linear order. Start with your low E, then top E, then A, then B, etc

Tools you'll need

To restring your guitar you'll need a set of wire/string cutters, a string winder, your new strings and a lint-free cloth for a quick clean

Line it up

As you start to tighten up the slack on new strings, ensure they're aligned with the right grooves in your guitar's nut (above the first fret)

03 Round the peg

Make sure the string is aligned with the grooves in your guitar's neck, then wind the top part of your new string around its corresponding tuning peg and push the rest through its hole to ensure it stays in place.

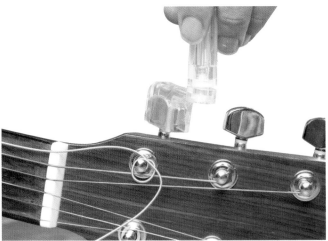

04 Wind and repeat

To stop the string from unravelling from the tuning peg, use a string winder to tune it up until the string is fairly taut. Repeat this process for all six strings, then your guitar will need to be tuned.

Hold your guitar

There are numerous ways to hold the guitar, but not all of them are conducive to good playing. Here we outline the best ways to hold your instrument

Your posture while playing the guitar is vitally important because if you slouch or are generally seated badly, then you could easily pick up bad playing habits that could make it much harder to learn to play.

When learning, the best position is to remain seated with a nice straight back, with your strumming hand resting over the sound hole or pickups and the thumb of your fretting hand pressed against the neck of your instrument so that your fingers have more flexibility to reach around

and press down on the strings. As your confidence grows, however, you can play your instrument while standing up too. Many guitar players prefer to stand while performing but we recommend working your way up to it. And it's not just deciding whether to stand or sit with your guitar; there are also two different hand positions when holding the neck. In this tutorial we provide useful tips on ensuring that your guitar-playing doesn't suffer through lack of comfort, whichever way you choose to play.

Correct hand position

There are two ways to hold the neck

When learning, you'll probably be told that the best way to hold the neck of your guitar is to press your thumb against the back of the neck. This will allow your fingers to crane over the fretboard and enable you to press down on the strings much more easily. However, the more you play, you may find it more natural to rest your thumb on top of the neck. Either way is fine, and although the method of resting your thumb on the neck might restrict the movement of your fretting fingers, doing so will allow you to bring your thumb around and use it as an unorthodox fretting tool.

The orthodox position, with thumb on back of neck

Sitting with your guitar

The ideal position to maintain while seated with your instrument

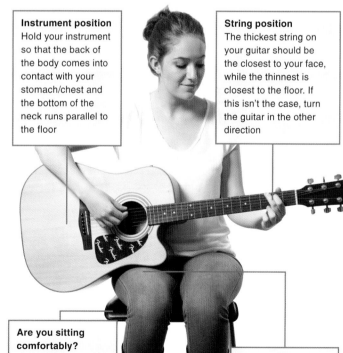

Instrument position
Hold your instrument so that the back of the body comes into contact with your stomach/chest and the bottom of the neck runs parallel to the floor

String position
The thickest string on your guitar should be the closest to your face, while the thinnest is closest to the floor. If this isn't the case, turn the guitar in the other direction

Are you sitting comfortably?
Sit in an armless chair and be seated with your back against the back of the chair. Slouching is a definite no-no as it could lead to you developing bad habits

Rest on your far leg
The body of the guitar will rest on one of your legs. In most styles of playing, the guitar will rest on the leg farthest away from the headstock

Standing with your guitar
Don't sacrifice your comfort while you stand up to play your instrument

When learning guitar, it is natural to sit down with your instrument as this allows you to concentrate more on your playing and less on your body movement. And while any time spent practising is good, you might find that standing allows you to be more mobile, helps your playing posture and forces you to concentrate on your chords without looking at them. Plus it's infinitely more 'rock 'n' roll' than sitting, right? So here are some useful tips for playing your instrument while standing.

"With the strap on your shoulder, stand with your back against a wall to get an understanding of how straight you should stand"

Weigh it up
Good posture is what allows you to stand while playing guitar. You probably already know how to sit while practising, so practise standing with your back nice and straight. Hold your guitar in your hand and walk around with it strapped to you so that your body gets used to the weight.

Adjust your strap
Make sure that your strap sits on your shoulder and not on the end of your shoulder. The latter will cause the strap to dig in and become uncomfortable. With the strap placed correctly on your shoulder, stand with your back against a wall to get a better understanding of how straight you need to stand.

Keep it centred
Most electric guitars have a cut-away section in the middle so that the body of your instrument fits right up against your body under your ribs. Stand up straight and don't slump your shoulders, arch your back and stick your chest out; this allows your guitar to be centred at your core.

Get the height right
Your guitar cannot be hanging too low or too high in relation to your body. When finding the perfect height for your fretting hand, make sure that you can access every fret equally. If you have to uncomfortably contort your fingers to do so then that's a good indicator that your position isn't good.

Strumming hand
Your strumming hand should rest comfortably on the side of your guitar's body and have easy access to all of the strings. If your guitar is too high you will have to twist your wrist one way, and if it's too low you'll have to twist it the other way. Playing this way could cause you some damage.

Playing aids
There are a wide range of accessories available to aid your playing position

Guitar straps
Guitar straps come in a wide range of styles and colours, all of which can be adjusted to a height that suits you and feels comfortable while playing.

Quick-release straps
Some straps, like Dimarzio's ClipLock range, feature clips that enable the main strap to be detached from the locking sections that remain on the guitar.

Footstools
To aid comfortable sitting, footstools, such as the FretRest by Proline, can be set to raise your guitar up on your knee to optimum height.

Hold your pick

An alternative to picking your strings with your fingers is to use a guitar pick. In this tutorial we show you how to brandish this to strum your strings with ease

Whether you're a learner or a seasoned pro, you will undoubtedly benefit from using picks.

Playing guitar with a pick (or plectrum) produces a brighter, more vibrant sound than using your fingers. A pick also provides a greater contrast in tone across different plucking locations. For example, the difference in sound between playing a string close to the bridge and near the neck is greater.

Guitar picks can vary in thickness to accommodate different playing styles and types of strings. Thinner picks tend to offer a wider range of sounds, whereas thicker picks can produce a brighter tone. The thickness of the pick can also directly benefit you in

achieving your desired sound — such as thinner picks for rock and metal and thicker picks for jazz and blues. Guitar picks are generally made from plastic or nylon, but can also be made out of rubber, metal or glass, and are traditionally shaped like an isosceles triangle with two equal corners and a rounded third corner.

There are many ways for a guitarist to hold a pick while playing. For example, guitarists playing solos will often hold the pick between their thumb and index finger as this makes it easier to pick out individual notes from the strings. But in this tutorial we will show you a dependable way to hold a pick in order to achieve a clean strumming sound on your instrument.

Start picking
The best way to hold your pick for strumming

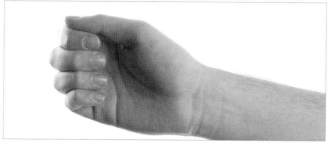

01 Correct hand position
Open your picking hand and turn the palm to face you. Close your hand to make a loose fist, ensuring that your thumb rests on the side of your index finger instead of on top of it.

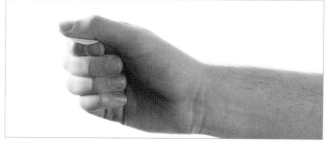

02 Place your pick
With your other hand, slide your guitar pick between your thumb and index finger so that the pick sits just behind the knuckle of your thumb. Make sure that the pointed end is pointing away from your fist.

03 Position over strings
Ensure that about half an inch of the pick is protruding from your fist. Position your picking hand over the sound hole of an acoustic guitar or the pickups of an electric guitar, so that it is hovering over the strings.

04 Strum the strings
Now move your wrist in a pendulum-like motion from your elbow and practise hitting the strings in a downward and upward motion. If they rattle excessively, try striking them softer or with less of the pick surface.

Holding your pick correctly
This method is ideal for getting clean and even contact on all of your guitar strings

TOP TIP

Get the right consistency
Holding the pick in this manner may feel strange at first, but it's ideal for getting good, even contact on your strings. Try to create fluidity in your picking; your downstrokes should sound near identical to your upstrokes.

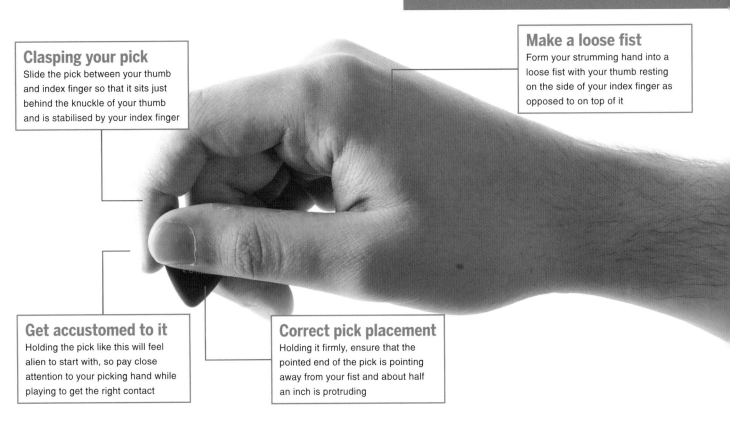

Clasping your pick
Slide the pick between your thumb and index finger so that it sits just behind the knuckle of your thumb and is stabilised by your index finger

Make a loose fist
Form your strumming hand into a loose fist with your thumb resting on the side of your index finger as opposed to on top of it

Get accustomed to it
Holding the pick like this will feel alien to start with, so pay close attention to your picking hand while playing to get the right contact

Correct pick placement
Holding it firmly, ensure that the pointed end of the pick is pointing away from your fist and about half an inch is protruding

Types of picks
Different picks suit different styles

Guitar picks vary in thickness to accommodate different playing styles and types of strings. Thinner picks are more flexible and tend to offer a wider, more dynamic range of sounds (from soft to loud) and are favoured by beginners, however, they will wear down quickly when compared to thicker ones. Thicker picks tend to allow for greater control over thicker gauge strings, such as those favoured by jazz guitarists. When buying a pick, they are referred to by their gauge, which essentially means their thickness. For instance a 0.73 pick is 0.73mm thick, a 1.5 pick is 1.5mm thick and so on.

Most picks are made of plastic, but you can get them in other materials too, such as stone which is inherently heavy and has no flexibility. You can also get different shapes and sizes, such as sharp-edged, to make it easier to pick the strings.

Experiment with different picks to find the one that best suits your playing style and guitar.

Strum your guitar

Strumming is one of the most basic, but crucial, aspects of learning to play the guitar. Here's how to get comfortable and confident with this key technique

> *"It's not uncommon to find it difficult to strum up and down comfortably"*

Strumming seems so simple, but there is an art to it. It's not uncommon to sit down with a guitar for the first time and find it difficult to strum up and down the strings comfortably. Most beginners tighten up their wrist, almost raking the strings, making it impossible to get any type of natural flow.

First and foremost, you need the right guitar pick. As we're just starting out, a thin pick — around 0.73mm — is best. It will allow far more freedom when performing downstrokes and upstrokes, giving you much more leeway when trying to ensure the same amount of pressure is applied to each. See the previous tutorial for the best way to hold a pick.

With your first attempt it's important to remember to keep your strumming arm moving up and down in a constant motion even if you're not hitting the strings. Doing this will get your mind into a rhythm of how to perform both the up and downstroke. Strum from the elbow too, and not the wrist, which should always be relaxed and never tight. Finally, don't fall into the trap of being overly nervous with your strumming and barely touching the strings. The idea is to hit them as quickly as you can so you get the sound of them all ringing out at once. At the same time, make sure you're always in control. Use the following strumming patterns to get started and listen to the audio online to check how they should sound.

Strumming
How to strum upwards and downwards

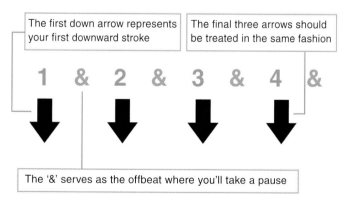

The first down arrow represents your first downward stroke

The final three arrows should be treated in the same fashion

1 & 2 & 3 & 4 &

The '&' serves as the offbeat where you'll take a pause

01 Downward strumming
The first step to comfortable strumming is perfecting the downstroke. This is simply taking the pick and strumming it down the strings. Start a gentle four count in your head or out loud, adding an 'and' between each number to represent the offbeat. For example, one and two and three and four, then repeat. Every time you say a number, strum down on the guitar and ensure you keep the rhythm. It may help to tap your foot at the same time as each number. Listen to the audio file included online to hear how it should sound.

02 Upward strumming
In order to play many of your favourite songs or simply get better at the guitar, it's imperative to perfect the upward stroke too. Using the same method described in Step 01, start the one and two and three and four rhythm again, only this time strumming up on the guitar every time you think or say the '&'.

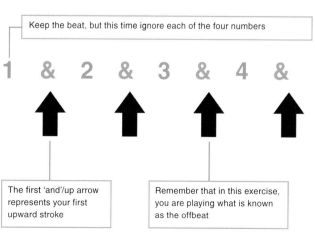

Keep the beat, but this time ignore each of the four numbers

1 & 2 & 3 & 4 &

The first 'and'/up arrow represents your first upward stroke

Remember that in this exercise, you are playing what is known as the offbeat

The perfect strumming technique
How to get it right from the start

TOP TIP

Tie it in
If you're struggling or lacking inspiration, try strumming along to your favourite song. Although the notes may not be correct, it'll help you learn how to keep time and when to perform up and downstrokes.

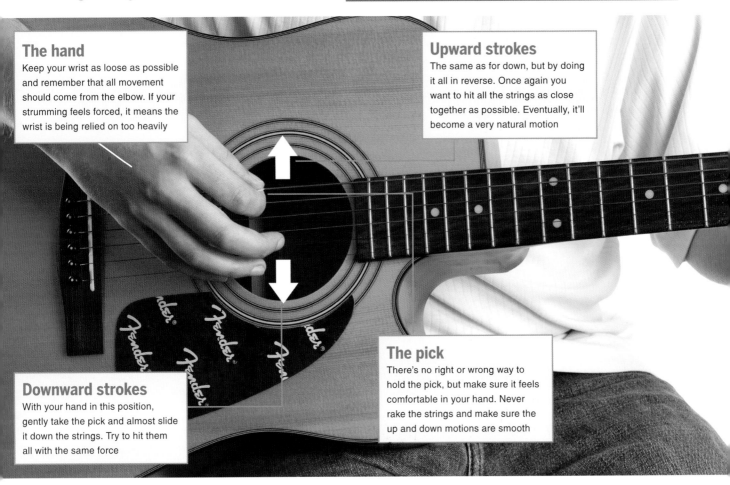

The hand
Keep your wrist as loose as possible and remember that all movement should come from the elbow. If your strumming feels forced, it means the wrist is being relied on too heavily

Upward strokes
The same as for down, but by doing it all in reverse. Once again you want to hit all the strings as close together as possible. Eventually, it'll become a very natural motion

Downward strokes
With your hand in this position, gently take the pick and almost slide it down the strings. Try to hit them all with the same force

The pick
There's no right or wrong way to hold the pick, but make sure it feels comfortable in your hand. Never rake the strings and make sure the up and down motions are smooth

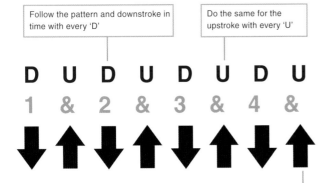

Follow the pattern and downstroke in time with every 'D'

Do the same for the upstroke with every 'U'

Keep doing the exercise until it becomes comfortable

03 Upward and downward strumming
Once again, follow the rules laid out in the other two steps, but this time go up and down on the guitar in one motion. You should strum down on the guitar on each number, and strum back up on the guitar on each '&'. Once you get more confident, you can even start to double up on certain strums.

04 Different beat strumming
When the first three steps feel easy, follow the diagram below in order to experiment with a different rhythm. This time there will be gaps you'll have to observe and stick to in order to get the right beat and become even more comfortable with strumming patterns.

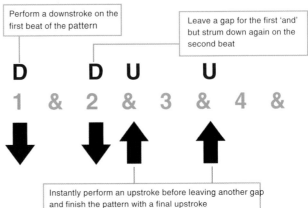

Perform a downstroke on the first beat of the pattern

Leave a gap for the first 'and' but strum down again on the second beat

Instantly perform an upstroke before leaving another gap and finish the pattern with a final upstroke

Warm up your hands

Warming up is key to playing well. Use these four quick exercises to get your hands loose, limber and ready to rock

Warming up your hands before you begin playing your guitar is crucial, which is why you'll see all the top pros do it. It brings a number of advantages, including helping to prevent RSI (repetitive strain injury), enabling you to move your hands and fingers more quickly and avoiding cramp while you're playing. Getting your hands used to the feeling of the frets will also give you the advantage of muscle memory when it comes to learning complicated riffs. Basically, a five-minute warm-up before you get into the trickier pieces will help you get the most out of your playing session and make you a better guitar player in the long run. And that's equally important whether you're getting on stage to rock out to thousands of people or just practising in your bedroom.

This guide will give you four quick exercises to get your muscles and joints warm, loose and agile, ready for your more challenging practices and performances. These exercises might not come

naturally or extremely easily to you at first, but soon they will be like second nature and you will be able to run them off as soon as you're tuned up and sitting comfortably. We will begin with basic chromatic exercises, which run up the notes a semitone at a time, and the last one is ideal for finger pickers as it stretches out and warms up your other hand too. You can listen and play along by opening the audio file provided online at FileSilo. Once you've got the hang of them, use a metronome to keep the pace of your playing even and then increase the speed to push yourself once you get comfortable. If you don't have a metronome, you can look to download a free app for your smartphone or tablet, if you have one. There are plenty to choose from.

TOP TIP
Keep warm
As well as flexible and stretched, your hands need to be warm. Avoid playing in very cold places (this will help keep your guitar in tune too), otherwise wear fingerless gloves so your playing doesn't suffer.

Get your hands ready
Why it's a crucial practice

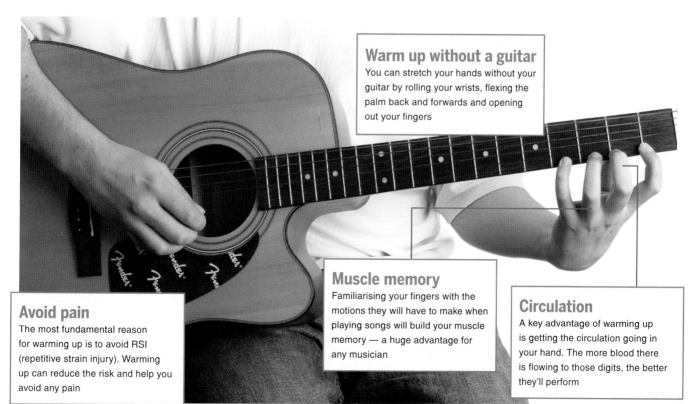

Warm up without a guitar
You can stretch your hands without your guitar by rolling your wrists, flexing the palm back and forwards and opening out your fingers

Muscle memory
Familiarising your fingers with the motions they will have to make when playing songs will build your muscle memory — a huge advantage for any musician

Circulation
A key advantage of warming up is getting the circulation going in your hand. The more blood there is flowing to those digits, the better they'll perform

Avoid pain
The most fundamental reason for warming up is to avoid RSI (repetitive strain injury). Warming up can reduce the risk and help you avoid any pain

Exercises to warm up
Stretch your hands and fingers

01 Chromatic steps
Starting on the low E string, place your index, middle, ring and little fingers on the first, second, third and fourth frets. Pluck the string once for each note, moving up and removing a finger each time. Repeat for all strings.

02 Chromatic pairs
Pluck low E with your index finger on the first fret, then with your middle finger on the second. Repeat for all strings, then change to middle and ring fingers on second and third frets. Carry on until you've used all your fingers.

03 Across the fretboard
Use the same finger pattern as the first exercise, but spread your fingers across the fretboard, your index finger starting on the low E on the first fret, your middle on the second string and second fret and so on.

04 Finger-picking warm-up
Put your fretting index finger on the third fret of the thick E and your ring finger on the third fret of the thin E. Follow the above tab and pluck using the pattern thumb, second, first, third, second, fourth, first, third, thumb.

Techniques

Learn how to play basic chords, the secret behind finger picking, and how your computer, tablet and smartphone can help you practise and record

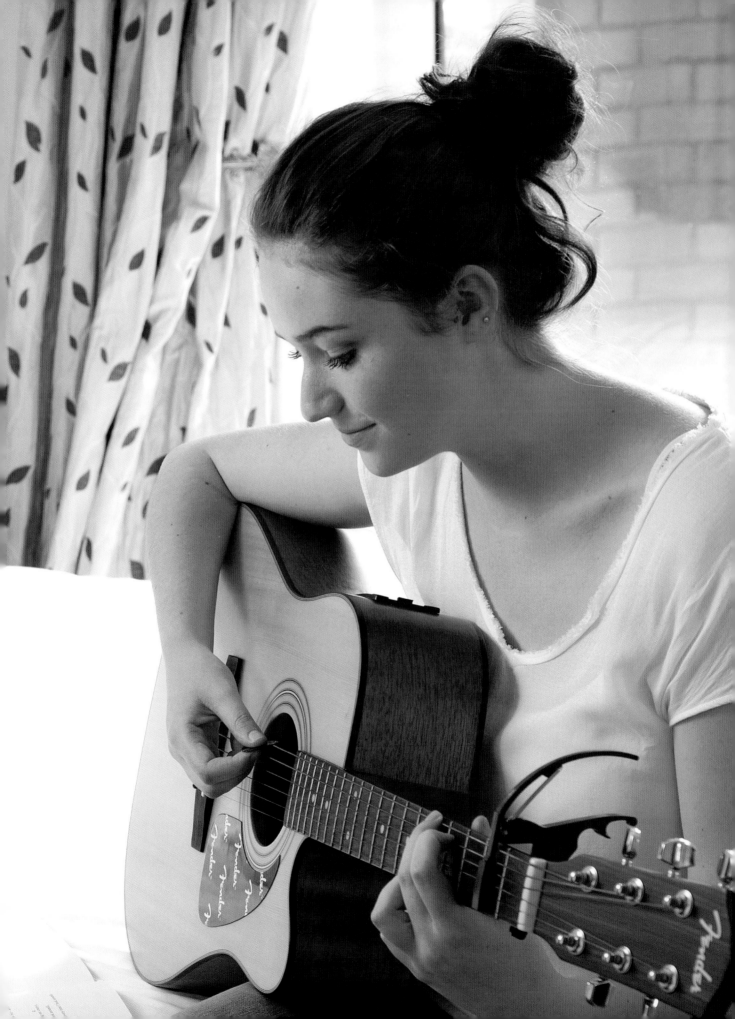

Notes, strings and frets

Music is made up of notes, and knowing where to find these notes on the neck of a guitar is vital if you are to develop as a player. Here, we show you how and where to find them

Notes form the tapestry of guitar playing. All music is made up of notes, and a note is just any pitch made by a musical instrument. Every note is symbolised by a letter, and the musical alphabet is made up of 12 notes: A, A#/B♭, B, C, C#/D♭, D, D#/E♭, E, F, F#/G♭, G, and G#/A♭ — after which the sequence goes back to the beginning and starts at A again, only an octave higher. The fretboard of a guitar is laid out so that you can find the notes on the neck by fretting the strings, and the same notes can be found at multiple places along the neck.

When learning where the notes on a guitar neck are located, it is useful to know that most natural notes (notes that aren't flats or sharps) are a whole two frets apart. The exceptions are between B and C, and E and F, as there is only a semitone between these notes. An F is made when fretting the first fret of either E string, but a G is created when playing the third fret. The notes in between are sharp or flat notes that are one semitone higher or lower than the previous note. For example, the note on the second fret of the E string is F#/G♭, as it's one fret higher than F, but one fret lower than G.

It is important to know where each note can be found on the neck so that you can play certain songs. It's worth remembering that certain notes sound better when played an octave higher, so finding your way around and experimenting with different notes is vital to your progression.

> *"It's worth remembering that certain notes sounds better when played an octave higher"*

Learning the open strings
Know what the open string notes are

The first thing you should know when learning guitar are the note names of the open strings. They are often used to describe finger placement (eg put your index finger on the second fret of the A string) and are also useful for tuning your guitar to another instrument. The diagram above shows the note names of the open guitar strings.

Note-finding tips
Here are some hints for how to remember string names and find specific notes

01 Remember the open string notes
The note names from the thinnest E string to the thickest E string can be easily remembered with quirky sayings like 'Easter Bunny Gets Drunk After Easter'. Whatever method you use to remember, knowing the strings off-by-heart is essential to being able to pick up and play.

02 Learn the musical alphabet
The musical alphabet is made up of only seven letters: A-G. This is because when we play the notes in order, the note that we would call 'H' sounds like another 'A', so the note is referred to as an 'A', only the pitch is higher. It is worth remembering that between the E and F, and B and C notes there is only one fret space between them.

03 Understand frets
Frets are the metal strips embedded along the fretboard of a guitar that divide the scale length. Pressing a string against a fret determines the string's vibrating length, and therefore its resultant pitch. The fret furthest along the neck is the first, and they get narrower as you get closer to the body.

04 Know what the root of a chord is
In music, the 'root' of a chord is the note or pitch upon which a chord may be built by stacking thirds. For example, a three-note triad using C as a root would be C-E-G. The name of the root note normally denotes the chord, so a major chord built on C would be called a C-major chord.

05 Be aware of note progression
Apart from B-C and E-F, all natural notes are separated by a tone (two semitones), which translates to two frets on the fretboard. B-C and E-F are separated by one semitone (one fret).

Notes on a guitar fretboard
Knowing where to find the notes on a guitar neck is vital if you are to further your skills

String				3rd		5th		7th		9th			12th
1st	E	F	F#/Gb	G	G#/Ab	A	A#/Bb	B	C	C#/Db	D	D#/Eb	E
2nd	B	C	C#/Db	D	D#/Eb	E	F	F#/Gb	G	G#/Ab	A	A#/Bb	B
3rd	G	G#/Ab	A	A#/Bb	B	C	C#/Db	D	D#/Eb	E	F	F#/Gb	G
4th	D	D#/Eb	E	F	F#/Gb	G	G#/Ab	A	A#/Bb	B	C	C#/Db	D
5th	A	A#/Bb	B	C	C#/Db	D	D#/Eb	E	F	F#/Gb	G	G#/Ab	A
6th	E	F	F#/Gb	G	G#/Ab	A	A#/Bb	B	C	C#/Db	D	D#/Eb	E

The open strings
The open strings on a guitar are usually tuned to E, B, G, D, A and E (starting from the thinnest first string through to the fattest sixth)

Enharmonic notes
This refers to notes that have the same pitch, but are known by different names. Most common are A#/B♭, C#/D♭, D#/E♭, F#/G♭ and G#/A♭. Although rare, a B note may be referred to as C♭, and an E as F♭

Learning notes on a string
Taking the fat E string as an example, when fretted on the first fret, the note becomes F, then F# on the second fret, then G, G#, A, A#, B, C, C#, D, D#, E, F, F# and then back through the sequence again

Two dots
Every note on a guitar string repeats itself every 12 frets, which is why there are two dots on the twelfth fret. So the E string played on the twelfth is the same note as the open E, just one octave higher

Flats and sharps
You will have undoubtedly seen the symbols in relation to notes, but what does a flat or a sharp actually mean?

A 'sharp' in music means higher in pitch and, when present, the sharp symbol raises a note by a semitone. More specifically, in musical notation, sharp means 'higher in pitch by a semitone' (half step) and it is represented by a '#' symbol. On the other hand, when we refer to a 'flat' in music, we mean a decrease in pitch, and when you see the associated flat symbol ('♭') it means that the note is lowered by a semitone (half step). When sharps are applied to guitar, then, it simply means that the note you are playing is a half step higher than the natural note. For example, the top open string is E, but if you press your finger on the first fret then it becomes an F. Move up one more fret and it becomes F sharp. A flat is half a note lower than the natural note — so F sharp and G flat are the same note, as both notes are played on the second fret of the top string.

Sharps
Sharps are a half step higher than the normal note and are usually represented by a '#' symbol.

Flats
Flats are a half note lower than the normal note and are usually represented by a '♭' symbol.

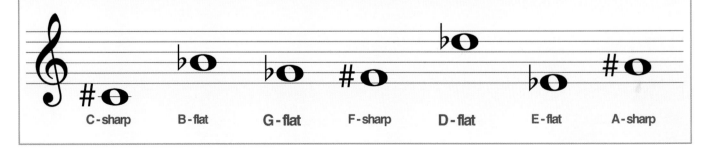

C-sharp   B-flat   G-flat   F-sharp   D-flat   E-flat   A-sharp

Play basic guitar chords

Learning these five basic chords is the first step on your guitar-playing journey. Practise often to master the art of switching notes

Guitar chords involve a collection of notes sounded together that are played on adjacent or separate strings, or all of the strings together. The guitar is a very versatile instrument for chording purposes, and there are five basic major chord patterns, which are C, A, G, E and D (known as the CAGED system). You may notice that there are some chords that appear to be missing, such as F and B (as well as the sharps and flats). Well, they aren't here because these chords don't have their own patterns — to play them you will have to use one of the basic patterns outlined here but with a barre applied.

When you first learn how to play chords, it can be difficult to get your fingers to co-operate, and you will undoubtedly feel some degree of discomfort as you press down on the strings, or generally as your fretting hand contorts into unnatural positions to fret the strings. However, before too long, with the aid of constant practice, your fingers will start to remember where to go. Other things to be aware of are a buzzing sound when you play the strings, which may indicate that you aren't pressing down on them hard enough, or that one or more of your fingers is catching a nearby string. When you strum the chord, each note should ring out clearly — if they don't do this then you need to quickly determine why. Some good tips include trimming the nails on your fretting hand so that they aren't impeding your contact with the fretboard, as well as ensuring that your fretting fingers are standing straight up and down so that they don't mute neighbouring strings. See pages 154-161 for the basic chords list.

> *"When you're first learning to play chords, it can be very difficult to get your fingers to co-operate"*

Fretting chords
Some things to be aware of when practising fretting basic chords

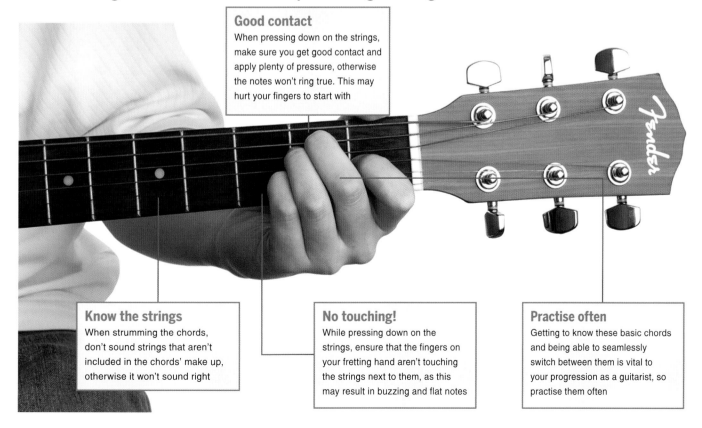

Good contact
When pressing down on the strings, make sure you get good contact and apply plenty of pressure, otherwise the notes won't ring true. This may hurt your fingers to start with

Know the strings
When strumming the chords, don't sound strings that aren't included in the chords' make up, otherwise it won't sound right

No touching!
While pressing down on the strings, ensure that the fingers on your fretting hand aren't touching the strings next to them, as this may result in buzzing and flat notes

Practise often
Getting to know these basic chords and being able to seamlessly switch between them is vital to your progression as a guitarist, so practise them often

G major
Fret and play the common G major chord

For this chord you need to press down on the fifth string (A) with your index finger at the second fret, the sixth string (low E) with your middle finger at the third fret, and the first string (high E) with your ring finger at the third fret. Now, strum all six strings together.

C major
Fret and play the common C major chord

For this chord you need to press down on the second string (B) with your index finger at the first fret, the fourth string (D) with your middle finger at the second fret and the fifth string (A) with your ring finger at the third fret. Now, strum all strings except the sixth (low E).

D major
Fret and play the common D major chord

For this chord you need to press down on the third string (G) with your index finger at the second fret, the first string (E) with your middle finger at the second fret and the second string (B) with your ring finger at the third fret. Now, strum the first four strings starting at D.

E major
Fret and play the common E major chord

For this chord you need to press down on the third string (G) with your index finger at the first fret, the fifth string (A) with your middle finger at the second fret and the fourth string (D) with your ring finger at the second fret. Now, strum all six strings together.

A major
Fret and play the common A major chord

For this chord press down on the fourth string (D) with your index finger at the second fret, the third string (G) with your middle finger at the second fret and the second string (B) with your ring finger also at the second fret. Now, strum all strings except the sixth (E).

TOP TIP

Keep your thumb out of the way
Although you may call upon the thumb of your fretting hand to fret certain notes on the sixth string as you become a more accomplished player, for now rest it out of the way on the back of the neck to allow your fingers to reach the strings more easily, especially for G.

Basic chord progression

Now it's time to get sore fingers. We will show you how to form basic chords and even recognise any song on the guitar by ear

As you will discover throughout this book, there are loads of guitar chords. Some are complicated and somewhat fiddly to learn, while others are relatively easy. Some chords will force you to contort the fingers of your fretting hand into unnatural positions, while others require just one finger.

A lot of chords take a long time to master, and others will take just a few minutes, but the important thing to remember is to take your time learning them and not try to rush yourself to learn them all at once because there are far too many for that.

In this tutorial we're going to teach you three basic chords — G major, C major and D major (commonly known simply as G, C and D). By mastering and using these three chords you will be able to figure out a song on the guitar by ear. Known as the '1-4-5' method (or I-IV-V), these chords represent chords #1, 4, and 5 in the key of G, the idea being that you think of any song and start playing with a simple downward strumming pattern while singing. When the chord you start with no longer fits the tone of the song, switch to another one of your three options until it fits, and then keep to this simple

method all the way through the song.

Keep practising these chords, visualising in advance where your fingers need to move to for the next chord and keeping your fingers nice and close to the fretboard so that you get a smooth transition without delaying the flow of the song.

Give it a try
Try this exercise to build your competence

Form the G-major chord with your fretting hand and strum the following pattern using only downstrokes (D). The lower line is for the beats and the '&' represents a short pause. So, as you count out the beat, insert an 'and' in between the numbers like this: one-and-two-and-three-and-four. When you have completed the fourth downward strum, change chord to C major and repeat the pattern before moving to D major. This gentle rhythm should give you plenty of time to find the correct chord. Move on to the next pattern when you feel confident.

D   D   D   D
1 & 2 & 3 & 4 &

The following pattern is similar to the first, but with upstrokes (U) where the '&' is in-between numbers, so there's less time to form chords.

D U D U D U D U
1 & 2 & 3 & 4 &

"Remember to take your time learning chords and not try to rush yourself"

Why do my chords not ring out properly?

Although you may call upon the thumb of your fretting hand to fret certain notes on the sixth string as you become a more accomplished player, for now rest it out of the way on the back of the neck to allow your fingers to reach the strings more easily, especially for G.

Learning the '1-4-5' method

Master these three basic chords and you'll be able to play your first song

D major

Place your index finger on the G (third) string, second fret, your middle finger on the E (first) string, second fret, and your ring finger on the B (second) string, third fret.

C major

Place your index finger on the B (second) string, first fret, your middle finger on the D (fourth) string, second fret, and your ring finger on the A (fifth) string, third fret.

G major

Place your index finger on the A (fifth) string, second fret, your middle finger on the E (sixth) string, third fret, and your ring finger (or little finger) on the E (first) string, third fret.

Play barre chords

They are the most painful chords to learn, but by far the most versatile once mastered. Here, we guide you through the basic hand positions

> *"The E-shape barre chords use all six strings, and are therefore easier to strum through"*

Put simply, barre chords hurt — at least they will while you're learning to play them, because they require you to contort your fretting hand into all kinds of unnatural positions as you press down on multiple strings with one finger.

There are two main categories of barre chords: those that use shapes from the family of open E chords (E major, E minor, E7 and so on) and those that use shapes from the family of open A chords.

The E-shape barre chords are probably the most popular, mainly because they use all six strings (like the open E chords that we've already learned). They are therefore easier to strum through as you don't have to worry about avoiding any strings. The A-shape barre chords are only five-strings wide, just like the A chords that we've already learned. You can use a single A-minor barre-chord shape to play any minor chord — only the fret at which the chord is played needs to be adjusted. You can also use an E-major barre-chord shape to play any major chord.

With both sets of barre chords, it gets progressively more difficult to play them the further up the neck you move, as the frets get progressively closer together. On acoustic guitars your fretting hand will wind up against the body of the guitar, so you will find that you physically can't go much further than the ninth or tenth fret. This ultimately proves not to be much of a problem, though, as any given chord can be found in many positions on a guitar, and before too long you will instinctively know where the best positions are.

Perfecting barre chords
Training your hands into the correct positions is a tricky process, but well worth the effort

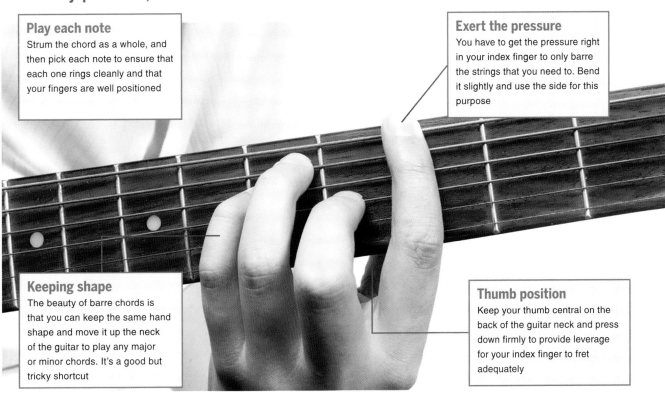

Play each note
Strum the chord as a whole, and then pick each note to ensure that each one rings cleanly and that your fingers are well positioned

Exert the pressure
You have to get the pressure right in your index finger to only barre the strings that you need to. Bend it slightly and use the side for this purpose

Keeping shape
The beauty of barre chords is that you can keep the same hand shape and move it up the neck of the guitar to play any major or minor chords. It's a good but tricky shortcut

Thumb position
Keep your thumb central on the back of the guitar neck and press down firmly to provide leverage for your index finger to fret adequately

Position your barring finger

A good trick to remember is to rotate your barring finger so that the knuckle is pointing towards the headstock you are barring with the side of your finger, thus avoiding missing strings with the natural kink in the middle.

Using the shape of E major

The shape outlined here is a major chord with the root on the sixth string. By moving this shape up the fretboard you can play any major chord

01 Fret an open E chord
Put your middle finger on the G string first fret, your ring finger on the A string second fret and your little finger on the D string second fret.

02 Move up two frets
Slide this hand position up the neck two frets, keeping your fingers on the same strings. Your index finger should be kept free.

03 Barre the strings
Now, crane your index finger over the neck and use it to press down on all of the strings at the second fret. This may take some practice.

Using the shape of A minor

The shape here is a minor chord with the root on the fifth string. When moved up the fretboard, you can use this shape to play any minor chord

01 Barre first five strings
Slightly bend your index finger and lay it flat across strings one to five on the second fret. Roll your finger back slightly towards the nut.

02 Position your fingers
Place your ring finger on D at the fourth fret, your little finger on G at the fourth fret, and your middle finger on B at the third fret.

03 Strum the chord
Strum the B-minor chord. Then, starting on the fifth string, play each string one at a time, making sure that each note rings clearly.

Using the shape of E minor

The shape here is a minor chord with the root on the sixth string. By moving this shape up the fretboard you can play any major chord

01 Barre all six strings
Bend your index finger on the third fret and lay it across all six strings. Make sure your thumb is placed firmly on the back of the neck.

02 Position your fingers
Put your ring finger on A at the fifth fret and the little finger on D at the fifth fret. Don't worry if you need to remove your barring finger for now.

03 Strum the chord
If you needed to remove your barring finger, place it back on the third fret. Strum this G-minor chord. All strings should ring clearly.

Barre chord tips

Now that you know the basics of barre chords, we provide a little extra assistance for helping you play them easier and more effectively

Nobody said that learning barre chords was going to be easy, right? Far from it, but as well as knowing the basic structures and hand positions that make up the chords, there are plenty of tricks you can implement to make playing them slightly less taxing.

Most of these boil down to your playing posture and the way in which you are holding the guitar. While learning these complex chords, you needn't worry about looking cool and adopting a rock 'n' roll stance — it's far more important and practical to get your body trained and getting used to the position it needs to be in so that you can fret the strings properly and get those barre chords sounding nice and clean.

The main thing to watch out for is your thumb position — you may forget about it if you're concentrating too hard on keeping your index finger held down across all the strings. Make sure that it's pressing the middle of the back of the neck, as this makes it far easier for your fretting fingers to reach the required frets.

Chord diagrams
How to read barre-chord diagrams for your finger positions

When learning to play any chord on your instrument, it is important to know the correct positions for your fingers in relation to the strings that you need to fret. The number '1' refers to your index finger, which is the finger that you'll use to hold down all six strings at the first fret for this barre chord (F major). Even though your index finger will be across all the strings, the '1' will not be written on the strings that have other fingers fretted on them — you can't play two notes on the same string during the same chord! The numbers '2', '3' and '4' refer to the middle, ring and little finger respectively. This is the E-major shape, although the fingers you would normally use have changed. This must all sound quite confusing at first but you'll be surprised at how practise really does make perfect when it comes to playing guitar.

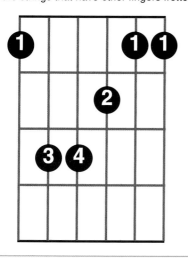

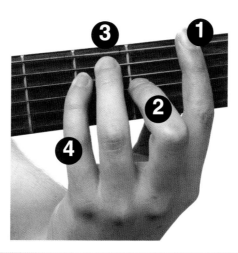

Give it a try
Practise barre chords with this strumming pattern

This exercise will help develop a rhythmic strumming technique and allow you to practise moving between the barre chords that use the shape of E major. To help with the timing of the strumming, try playing along with the audio file provided online. Just visit FileSilo to download the file so you can refer to it every time you need to practise.

Exercise details
Move through the barre chords that use the shape of E major while strumming. Start on the first fret, which forms an F-major barre chord, before moving over one string and up a fret to B minor then back across and up another fret to G major. Count to four, the numbers being downward strums, the 'ands' upward strums. After '4', refret to the E7-shape barre chord and repeat before the E-minor shape and Em7 shape barre chords.

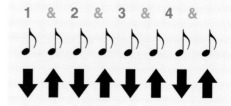

"There are plenty of tricks you can implement"

Practise frequently

As learning barre chords involves moving your hand and body, into unnatural positions, it certainly helps to practise every day — even if it's just for a couple of minutes. Concentrating on barre chords regularly will help develop your ability to place them in just a couple of weeks.

Tricks for better barre chords

Playing barre chords involves hours of practice, but these tips should get you off to the best start

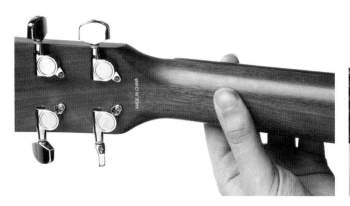

01 Check thumb placement

For any chords — barre chords especially — your thumb should be pressing against the back of the neck so that it is easier for you to crane your fretting fingers across the fretboard in order to reach all of the required strings.

02 Finger placement

Your index finger should be parallel with the fret wire, so close that it's barely touching the side. Roll your finger slightly towards the nut so that the bony side of the finger digs into the strings to help you get sufficient contact and force.

03 Don't press too hard

Your index finger is only responsible for fretting some of the strings, so don't try to press down on each string with equal force. When playing a standard barred F chord, press hard with the tip of your finger on the sixth string, and dig your knuckle into the first and second strings.

04 Get some leverage

Holding your guitar in the correct manner is vital for playing barre chords. If you hold your guitar too close to yourself you won't be able to get sufficient leverage on your fretting hand to barre the strings, so position it away slightly so that your hand can clamp down easier.

05 Move your elbow

In relation to the previous tip, place the elbow of your fretting hand closer to your body than you would otherwise do (at around waist level). This will enable your index finger to roll onto its side more, thus making it far more easier for you to hold down the strings.

Finger pick

"Basic finger-picking techniques can add another dimension to the chord"

Take your first steps in learning this distinctive style by following our simple finger-picking guide

Finger picking is the alternative to using a plectrum (pick) to pluck the strings of your guitar. It means you can play more than one note at a time and create rhythmic and melodic patterns for chords. It is typical of classical, folk and country guitar playing, usually using an acoustic instrument.

While you can learn to finger pick particular melodies and riffs, an ideal place to start is with a chord that you are already familiar with. Basic finger-picking techniques can take the exact same chord patterns and replace the strumming with picking that draws out individual notes or groups of notes. This can add another dimension to the chord, enabling you to vary the pace and feel of the music.

Before you start, it's very important to get the position of your picking hand right. It should rest naturally over the sound hole or pickup without your wrist having to bend or twist at all. Generally your thumb will play the lowest three notes (E, A and D in standard tuning) so make sure it's comfortable to do so. It's rare to pluck any strings with your little finger, so keep it relaxed and out of the way.

This tutorial will teach you a basic pattern to finger pick with the G major chord. Repeat this until you feel comfortable playing it relatively quickly, then try plucking the same strings with different chords held down on the fretboard. To start, download the video file from FileSilo.

Finger pick in G
Learn the basic pattern

01 The G chord
Hold the chord of G major (see the above picture and our chord guide on the next page). Strum to make sure all of the strings are held down then get your thumb ready on the root note, in this case the low E string.

02 Root and fifth
Pluck the low E and the B string together using your thumb and middle finger. Use the outer edges of your fingertips and try to get the volume of each string roughly the same.

03 Finger run
Using your index, second and third fingers, pluck the third, fourth and fifth strings in a running pattern, up and then back down (first finger, second, third, second, first). Play steps 2 and 3 together and repeat.

04 Practice makes perfect
Play this pattern until it feels natural. You can drop your finger on the fretboard on the low E string to play it on the second fret of the A and take it off completely as you repeat the pattern for variations on the G chord.

Learn to finger pick
What you need to know for a basic pattern

Hand position
Your hand should rest naturally over the sound hole (or pickup for electric guitars) without bending your wrist. The thumb usually rests on the lowest string

Plucking
To pluck the strings, use the outer edges of your fingertips and move as if beginning to make a fist, coming in towards each other and slightly away from the guitar

Adding variation
You may need to change the root note (what the thumb plays) to the second string for chords such as C major and A minor

Which fingers?
The thumb usually plays the three lowest notes (E, A and D strings) while your index, second and ring fingers play the rest. This can be adapted and is just a guide

Change chord
Pick between major and minor

When you have spent time practising and are comfortable with the basic picking pattern, you can use it to move between chords. G major works well with E minor, so pluck the strings exactly as in the four steps and then change your fingers on the fretboard to the E minor chord and continue. See our chord diagrams here on the right for how to play these two chords.

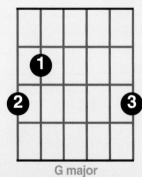

G major

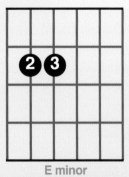

E minor

TOP TIP

Use your nails
Some players prefer just to use the tips of their fingers, but growing the nails on your plucking hand so they are just longer than your finger can help. The different surface can produce a clearer sound, especially for the

Play hammer-ons and pull-offs

Using this technique we show you how to create a smoother sound between two different notes using your fretting hand

For a hammer-on (also known as an upward slur), a note is plucked and then a second note is sounded by slamming (or 'hammering') another finger onto the same string at a higher fret. For example, if you place your index finger onto the first string (E) at the fifth fret, pluck the string with your strumming hand and then 'hammer' your middle finger down onto the first string on the sixth fret, you will perform a hammer-on and, in the process, create a pleasing sound between the notes.

A pull-off is essentially the opposite, so using the previous example, you will start with your index finger on the first string at the fifth fret, and your middle finger on the first string at the sixth fret. Pick the string with your strumming hand and pull your middle finger off shortly afterwards, but make sure your index finger is still on the fifth fret. Like the hammer-on, you should be able to hear two distinct notes, even though you've only picked one. Try pulling your index finger off after your middle finger. If you perform this successfully, you should hear an open E note. See how many notes you can pull off and hammer on until the sound fades out.

By incorporating these hammer-ons and pull-offs into your guitar playing, you'll achieve a smoother, more fluid sound.

How to hammer-on and pull-off
Achieve smoother sounds

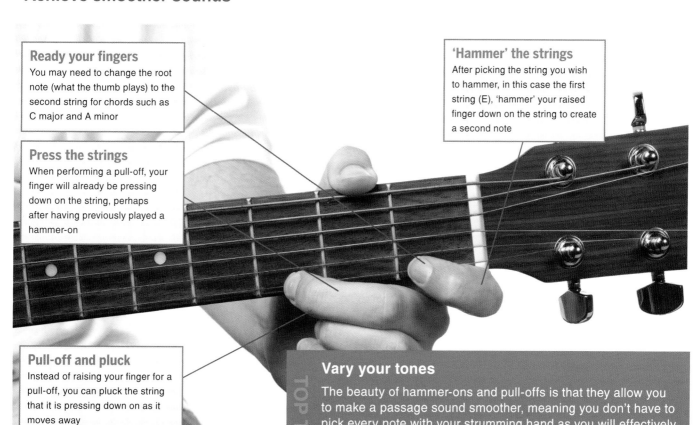

Ready your fingers
You may need to change the root note (what the thumb plays) to the second string for chords such as C major and A minor

Press the strings
When performing a pull-off, your finger will already be pressing down on the string, perhaps after having previously played a hammer-on

'Hammer' the strings
After picking the string you wish to hammer, in this case the first string (E), 'hammer' your raised finger down on the string to create a second note

Pull-off and pluck
Instead of raising your finger for a pull-off, you can pluck the string that it is pressing down on as it moves away

TOP TIP

Vary your tones
The beauty of hammer-ons and pull-offs is that they allow you to make a passage sound smoother, meaning you don't have to pick every note with your strumming hand as you will effectively be plucking strings with both hands. With experience, you can learn to play very fast using these techniques.

Playing hammer-ons and pull-offs
Perfect your technique

01 Get ready to hammer
Start off by positioning your index finger over — not touching — the first string at the first fret, and with your middle finger over — not touching — the first string at the third fret.

02 Perform the hammer-ons
Pick the open first string (E), hammer your index finger down on the first string at the first fret, and then quickly hammer your middle finger down on the first string at the third fret.

03 Straight into pull-offs
Now, in one swift sequence, pull your middle finger down off the first string at the third fret, perhaps plucking it as you go, and then pull your index finger down off the first string at the first fret.

04 Practise the sequence
When played quickly, the open note followed by the two hammer-ons, and then two pull-offs will form a sequence of notes that moves up and then back down a scale. Now, work on speed and fluidity.

Give it a try
Improve your technique using the exercise you practised with during this tutorial

Using the same hammer-on and pull-off exercise that we showed you here, practise trying it on different strings and while throwing different frets into the mix. Performing hammer-ons on any string is easy, but not quite so for pull-offs, as you need to exercise caution in order to avoid accidentally sounding the neighbouring strings, which can be a regular occurrence at first. With plenty of practice, however, mastering hammer-ons and pull-offs can be done.

Exercise details
Pick the open second string, hammer your index finger down on the second string, first fret, and quickly hammer your middle finger down on the second string, third fret. In a swift sequence, pull your middle finger down off the second string at the third fret, and your index finger down off the second string at the first fret. Repeat for all the strings.

Practice string bending

String bending was developed by blues and country players to mimic bottleneck guitars. Here's how to perfect this technique

String bending is a very basic blues and country technique that involves 'bending' or pushing the string over the fingerboard with your fretting fingers so that the string gets tighter and the pitch goes up.

Bending the strings far enough to get the pitch to change can take quite a bit of effort, especially for a novice, so the key is to use three of the fingers on your fretting hand to manipulate the string — one (your ring finger) on the fret you intend to bend and then a further two (your middle and index fingers) on the frets next to it for added leverage. However, if you have a tremolo arm for your guitar then you can also achieve the same bending effect mechanically.

The principle factor that dictates the degree in which you can bend a string is its thickness (or gauge). The width of a guitar string is expressed as a decimal fraction of an inch, and can be found on the packaging of the various strings available. Weighing up the pros and cons of each thickness is a matter of personal taste, but you

should be aware that while thin, light gauge strings are more pliable and easier on your fretting fingers, they are more likely to break with continued use, have a lower volume and are harder to keep in tune. Thicker strings provide a warmer tone and are a lot more durable, though certainly not as easy to bend. It's a good idea to experiment with as many gauges as possible when starting out to see what works for you.

> **TOP TIP**
>
> ### Maintain the note
>
> If the note is trailing off before you've completed the bend then you're probably not exerting enough pressure on the fretboard. Make sure you use all three fingers to push the string up towards the sky. It is easier to bend strings on higher frets.

How to bend your strings
Bend strings to change the pitch of a note

01 Position your fingers
Start off by placing your ring finger on the fret you wish to bend, in this case the second (B) string, tenth fret, and then place your middle and index fingers on the same string, but on the ninth and eighth frets.

02 Hear the pitch
The aim is to bend the note up one semitone then return the note to its original pitch. Play the second string (B) on the tenth fret and the same string on the eleventh fret so that you can hear the pitch of the note.

String bending
Change the pitch of the strings

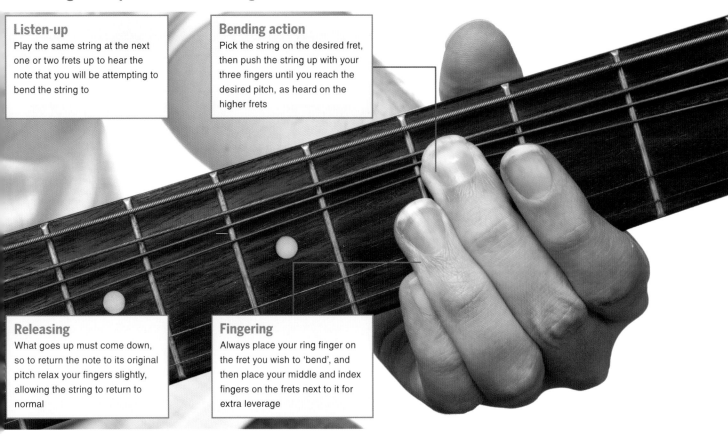

Listen-up
Play the same string at the next one or two frets up to hear the note that you will be attempting to bend the string to

Bending action
Pick the string on the desired fret, then push the string up with your three fingers until you reach the desired pitch, as heard on the higher frets

Releasing
What goes up must come down, so to return the note to its original pitch relax your fingers slightly, allowing the string to return to normal

Fingering
Always place your ring finger on the fret you wish to 'bend', and then place your middle and index fingers on the frets next to it for extra leverage

03 Execute the bend
Now, with your fingers in position as indicated in the first step, pick the second string (B) on the tenth fret and, using your three fingers, push the string up and 'bend' the note so that it sounds like the eleventh fret.

04 ...and relax
Once you have exerted enough pressure on the string to bend the pitch, relax your fingers slightly to allow the string to spring back down to its natural position and allow the note to return to its original pitch.

Mute strings

In this tutorial, we show you methods of blocking out unwanted noise when you want to concentrate on picking individual strings

String muting is a technique that is used to prevent certain strings from sounding while playing other strings. The reason why guitarists mute strings at times is because otherwise the vibrating strings will interfere with the music they're making. For example, when playing licks, the bending and release of a higher string will cause the lower bass strings to vibrate, either because they've been accidentally hit or because they've simply vibrated when other strings have been hit. To effectively mute strings that you don't want to be heard, there are numerous techniques available. For example, many players use the palm of their picking hand to mute the lower strings, which involves 'karate chopping' your hand down across the strings next to the bridge, placing your pick between your thumb and index finger, and moving the side of your hand up or down to mute the low strings. This technique is hard to get right, as the margin for keeping one string unmated and the others from vibrating is very slim. Another technique for muting the lower strings is to use the thumb of your picking hand, which rests on the lower strings as you pick the higher ones with your plectrum.

Then we come to the higher strings. Again, there are a couple of methods you can employ to stop the high notes from ringing out as you pluck the lower strings. If you have spare fingers on your fretting hand then you can rest those lightly on the strings on the frets. Alternatively, you can use the spare fingers of your picking hand. Whatever method you choose, you'll need to practise the technique thoroughly to get the results you crave.

Preventing unwanted noise
We examine the parts of your playing hands you can use

TOP TIP

Use palm muting when you can

It's tricky to get your palm in the perfect position to consistently and reliably mute strings adjacent to the one you're playing, and the palm takes more time to stop the string from ringing than your thumb, so try using that technique when possible.

Use your fingers
To mute high strings with your picking hand, use the fingers that aren't holding the pick to press against the strings

Use your thumb
You can also mute the low strings using the thumb of your picking hand. Rest the thumb against the low strings as you pick the high strings

Use the palm
An effective way to mute the low strings is to rest the palm of your hand across them, and then just raise it to free up the strings that you want to play

Fret muting
Alternatively, you can use spare fingers from your fretting hand to mute the strings on the neck, but don't press too hard, otherwise you'll fret them

How to mute your strings
We demonstrate the four main methods

01 Palm muting
Fashion your hand into a karate chop, and then place it just in front of the bridge of your guitar so that your hand is at a 90-degree angle to the strings. Now, move the side of your hand up or down to mute the strings.

02 Thumb muting
The disadvantage of muting with your thumb is that the pick is at rest away from the strings. Rectify this by muting the lower strings using the thumb of your picking hand so that the point of rest is not on the strings.

03 Fret muting
One technique for muting the higher strings is to use the underside of the index finger on your fretting hand. Press lightly — not too hard so as to 'fret' the strings — to mute the higher strings that you don't want to sound.

04 Finger muting
A good technique for muting higher strings is to use the otherwise unused fingers of your picking hand. Any fingers that aren't holding the pick, such as your middle, ring and little finger, can rest on the higher strings.

Learn to slide

Master how to transition between two notes or chords by sliding between them, and you'll open up many new possibilities

Sliding is a common technique used in many genres, enabling the guitarist to move between notes or power chords without lifting his or her hand from the guitar's fretboard.

All you need to do in order to execute a successful slide on your guitar is to play one note, then, without taking your fretting finger off the fretboard, slide it up to another fret. You won't have to pick the second note if your slide was good. As its name suggests, the effect it produces is a sliding sound. This technique makes a much smoother sound than what is produced by picking the two notes separately.

Slides are also very versatile. As well as sliding up, it is just as simple to slide down the other way. You can also play two or more notes at the same time and slide those fingers up or down the fretboard to create a similar sliding effect, but with chords. However, this technique takes a bit more practise, and we recommend having new strings on your guitar before trying it, as the grime and dirt that accumulates from years of playing can make sliding tough to pull off.

TOP TIP

Clean the strings

If sliding is proving tough, possibly because of old strings hindering your movement, try using a string cleaner like Fast Fret. It's cheap, it will clean your strings up, and it'll make it far easier for you to slide along.

Unlike hammer-ons and pull-offs (see pages 48-49), which rely on different fingers of your fretting hand, a slide should be made by the same finger or fingers that fretted the original note. Once you've mastered slides with your fingers, you could try using a steel or glass guitar slide instead, which should be available to buy at your local music shop. These are often used in blues compositions and produce a distinct sound to the one that can be heard in your source files. Go to FileSilo to download the audio files and a step-by-step video guide.

Sliding
Use your fingers to slide

01 Separate notes
Pick the note on the third fret of the A string (a C note in normal tuning). Then, after taking your finger off the fretboard, play the fifth fret on the same string (a D note). Remember the two separate sounds.

02 Slide between notes
Play the third of the A string again, but this time slide between the third and fifth fret without taking your finger off the fretboard. Hear how it should sound on the audio file provided.

Slide with your hands
Easily produce a sliding sound

"We recommend having new strings on your guitar before trying slides"

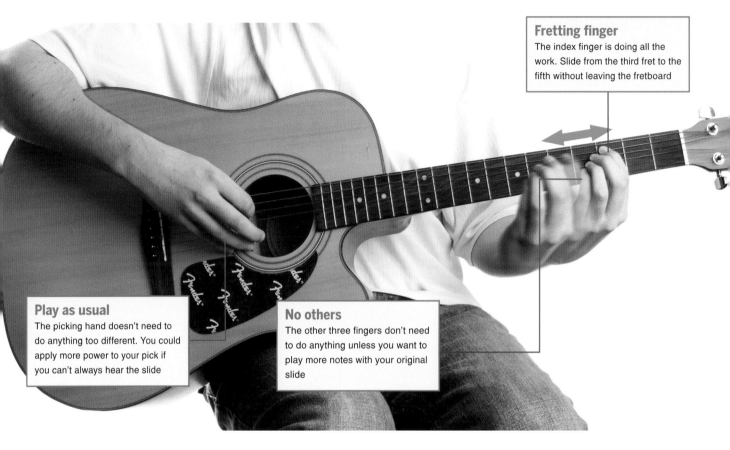

Fretting finger
The index finger is doing all the work. Slide from the third fret to the fifth without leaving the fretboard

Play as usual
The picking hand doesn't need to do anything too different. You could apply more power to your pick if you can't always hear the slide

No others
The other three fingers don't need to do anything unless you want to play more notes with your original slide

03 Slide with chords
Fret the third fret on the A string again, but this time add the fifth fret on the D to make a basic power chord. Play these two strings and slide both fingers up to the fifth and seventh on A and D respectively.

04 Try using a guitar slide
For an entirely different sound, try using a guitar slide. Move any one of your fretting fingers up and down the fretboard, playing the D, G, and B strings with your picking hand.

Use natural harmonics

Create a clear, bell-like sound from your acoustic or electric guitar with the correct finger positioning and a light touch on the strings

I f you want to make your acoustic or electric guitar play a completely different sound, try using natural harmonics.

If you want to make your acoustic or electric guitar play a completely different sound, try using natural harmonics.

The key to achieving a successful and effective natural harmonic is the positioning of your fretting finger. Rather than pushing your finger down on the string as you would when playing a regular note, you must only rest your finger on the top of the string without applying downward pressure. When played correctly, a natural harmonic, like an open string, can still be heard even when playing another note (as long as it's on a different string).

The great thing about harmonics is that they're not limited to a

> *"The key to achieving an effective natural harmonic is the positioning of your fretting finger"*

genre. Popular guitarists, from blues and metal to folk and classical, have used them to add another dimension to their work. Listen to Genesis' Horizons to hear how harmonics can be played to produce a pleasant ringing sound in a solo acoustic song.

Harmonics can also be used for tuning purposes. As they ring (ie they don't stop when another note is played), a natural harmonic can be compared to a note played normally to see if the guitar is in tune. The simplest and most commonly used harmonics can be played on the twelfth, seventh and fifth frets, but with practice you will soon be able to play natural harmonics all over the fretboard. However, be warned that some are a lot harder to achieve than others.

A different sound
Play different natural harmonics

01 Your first harmonic
On the twelfth fret, rest your fretting index finger on the low E string. Pick the string and it should ring even if you lift your finger. Hear how a twelfth fret harmonic on the low E string should sound on the audio files provided.

02 Tune with harmonics
Play the same harmonic as in Step 1, but while that note is ringing, play the seventh fret as normal on the A string. If your guitar is in tune, the notes should sound the same.

Achieving harmonics
Don't apply any pressure

Above the seventh
You'll get the best ring to your harmonics if you rest your fretting finger directly above the fret rather than in between frets

No pressure
To achieve a natural harmonic, you must not push your fretting finger down on the string as you would when playing a normal note

Pick as normal
You need not do anything different with your picking hand. Try just picking the harmonic as you would a normal note

Keep them off!
As when you are playing a regular note, make sure your other fingers aren't touching the string you're playing

03 The seventh fret
On the D string, use the same technique as in Step 1, but above the seventh fret. You should hear a note with a higher pitch. Try moving from the twelfth fret to the seventh. You can do this on all strings except B.

04 Multiple harmonics
Harmonics aren't limited to one note. Rest your whole finger across the seventh fret of the guitar and strum the D, G, and B strings. This should give a pleasant-sounding chord of harmonics, as heard in your audio files.

Use a capo

Altering the pitch of your guitar is easy using a capo, and there are a wide variety of types to suit your instrument and style

A capo is the name for a small clamp that sits on the fretboard of your guitar, depressing all of the strings. It acts in the same way as a finger, taking the pitch higher. Each fret represents a semitone, so if you place a capo on the second fret, each string will sound a tone higher.

With a capo, you can play songs in a different key without having to relearn them or know anything about the intricacies of key signatures. Simply clamp on your capo and away you go. This can be really useful if you're adapting your piece to accompany other musicians, or if you want to sing along but the pitch of the music is too low or too high. They are useful for beginners, as you can adapt a piece you want to learn if the chord shapes used are too difficult. Barre chords, for example, can be deftly avoided. These are the chords where you use your index finger to press down on all six strings as part of the chord pattern . In standard tuning, B is a typical example of this. By placing your capo on the second fret, you can play the same chord progression (albeit in a different pitch), and to produce the equivalent of B you can use the easier A major chord pattern (see the chart on the right).

> *"A capo acts the same way as a finger, taking the pitch higher"*

Chord patterns

This chart shows how you can use your capo to transpose pieces into other keys. The left-hand column represents the original chord from your tablature or sheet music, and the subsequent chords are the shapes you should substitute it with depending on where your capo is.

Original chord	What a chord becomes when a capo is on fret number...							
	1	2	3	4	5	6	7	8
A		G		F	E		D	
A#/B♭	A		G		F	E		D
B		A		G		F	E	
C	B		A		G		F	E
C#/D♭	C	B		A		G		F
D		C	B		A		G	
D#/E♭	D		C	B		A		G
E		D		C	B		A	
F	E		D		C	B		A
F#/G♭	F	E		D		C	B	
G		F	E		D		C	B
G#/A♭	G		F	E		D		

Different types of capos

Choose the right one for your guitar and style

The kind of capo that's right for you depends on how much you're looking to spend, how you want it to work and what kind of guitar you have. There are many options, but here are three of the best:

01 The spring-loaded capo
This inexpensive option is one of the most commonly used types of capo. They can be operated easily with one hand, and can be applied or removed extremely quickly, even mid-song if need be. They can be quite strong, so are not suitable for instruments with wide necks or particularly low actions.

02 The smart capo
Working on an automatic mechanism, place this capo around your guitar neck and simply squeeze to clamp it in place. Applying pressure on the tips then releases it. These are very user-friendly, but can be expensive, and it's sometimes difficult to get them sitting tight enough on the first try.

03 The toggle capo
Another bargain option, these capos come in a range of styles and are generally small and portable. Ideal for wider-necked classical guitars, they have a tendency to pull strings out of tune because of the way they tighten, and can also stick to the strings after being undone.

Change the pitch
Use your capo for quick pitch changes

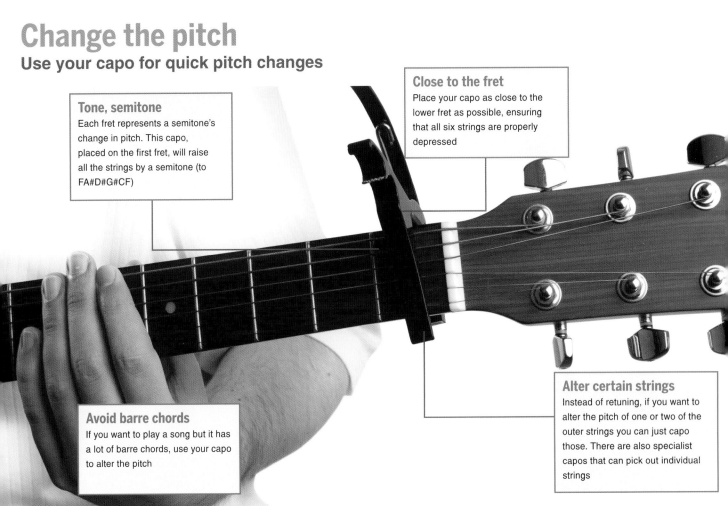

Tone, semitone
Each fret represents a semitone's change in pitch. This capo, placed on the first fret, will raise all the strings by a semitone (to FA#D#G#CF)

Close to the fret
Place your capo as close to the lower fret as possible, ensuring that all six strings are properly depressed

Avoid barre chords
If you want to play a song but it has a lot of barre chords, use your capo to alter the pitch

Alter certain strings
Instead of retuning, if you want to alter the pitch of one or two of the outer strings you can just capo those. There are also specialist capos that can pick out individual strings

Attach a capo
Make the most of this simple device

01 Attach your capo
Depending on your type of capo, open it and clamp it onto the neck of your guitar. Place it closer to the lower fret, as that is where the pitch change will come from.

02 Adjust to play
Strum without placing any fingers on the fretboard to see how it sounds, listening out for buzzing or muted notes. Check that all of the strings under the capo are lying straight, adjusting the position of the capo if needed.

Use an amp

It's not just the guitar that's needed to achieve the perfect sound. Say hello to another vital component…

It's easy to dismiss amplification when first starting to learn the guitar, putting all your faith in the make and type of instrument you buy instead. In reality, the two have to work in perfect harmony to achieve the sound you're looking for. Beginners are best starting off with a 'combo', an amp that combines the head and amplification cabinet into one, making it both easier to setup, understand and carry around. It's very likely that the first amp you purchase — assuming you don't spend a tremendous amount of money — won't achieve the tone you're looking for, but the key is to experiment with settings such as bass, trebles and mid to see what

takes your fancy. If a heavier sound is needed, it's gain, rather than volume, that should be your next step. All amps will come with clean and distorted channels, and increasing the gain for the latter is where the harsher, more edgy tones will come from. It makes sense to start with a practice amp early on, as it won't be as intimidating and will allow you to experiment with your likes and dislikes. Your setup can evolve to the point where you'll want a specific amp head — where you can control the sound and tone — and a cabinet to complement that.

Setting up
The basics of amplification

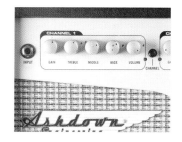

01 Clean sound

Most amps will be pre-programmed to the clean channel when you initially get them, and it's likely the options will revolve around bass, treble and volume. The sound may be slightly dry, but you always have the option to use any built-in effects or purchase an FX pedal.

02 Heavy sound

Getting a decent heavy sound is always going to be a challenge on a beginner's amp, but you will usually be able to fiddle with gain, bass, volume and contour/treble. Naturally, heavier tones will come from upping the gain, but balancing the other options is just as important.

03 Switching channels

Most guitar players, at one point or another, will want to switch between their pre-readied distorted and clean sounds. This is easily achieved by hitting a button on the amp or, more easily, buying a foot switch that can be plugged into most amps and requires only a little setup.

Top amps
Make the right purchase choice

Marshall MG30CFX
Easy to understand and to get to grips with, this combo Marshall amp will teach you the basics about amplification without throwing too much at you.

Fender Mustang II V.2
Incredibly simple and accessible, the real selling point here is the ability to save presets and certain sounds, despite its cheap price point. Well worth a look at when choosing an amp.

Blackstar Fly 3 Battery Powered Practice Amp
If you just need something to kick out some noise then this affordable 3 watt practice amp fits the bill. It features two channels (Clean and Overdrive) and a digital 'tape' delay effect.

Peavey Vypyr 15
Again the tone won't be the best, but the Vypyr 15 model has 24 channel models built-in to the amp so you can hear what more powerful and famous amps sound like.

Amplification basics
Why each setting is so important

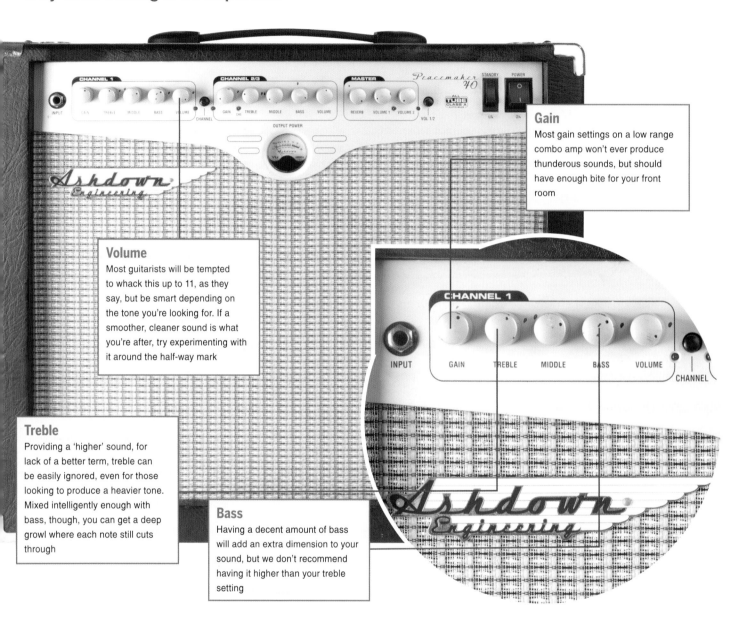

Gain

Most gain settings on a low range combo amp won't ever produce thunderous sounds, but should have enough bite for your front room

Volume

Most guitarists will be tempted to whack this up to 11, as they say, but be smart depending on the tone you're looking for. If a smoother, cleaner sound is what you're after, try experimenting with it around the half-way mark

Treble

Providing a 'higher' sound, for lack of a better term, treble can be easily ignored, even for those looking to produce a heavier tone. Mixed intelligently enough with bass, though, you can get a deep growl where each note still cuts through

Bass

Having a decent amount of bass will add an extra dimension to your sound, but we don't recommend having it higher than your treble setting

Orange CR120H Crush Pro Series 120 Watt Head

This high power, solid-state amp features two channels, digital reverb and packs an incredible 120 watts into a head with a great sound that Orange is strongly linked with.

Vox amPlug 2 Headphone Amp

For beginners or the individual who isn't allowed loud music in their house, Vox's headphone amp enables you to practice on an electric guitar without disturbing anybody in your area.

Use the right lead

TOP TIP

Beginner guitarists need not worry to any great degree, but the type of lead you use to connect your guitar to an amp can be extremely important, not only improving the quality of the sound that's emitted, but by being far more reliable.

Use effects

From distortion to delay, a guitar's sound can be drastically transformed thanks to an effects pedal

t's widely assumed that an effects pedal can get any tone or sound you need. While they are certainly beneficial and essential if you are looking for something specific, it's far more likely that any pedal will need to be used in conjunction with numerous other pieces of kit to be a true success. That doesn't mean they can't shape your education. Effects pedals are designed to boost certain tones or sound. The most common are distortion pedals, but effects such as chorus, delay and compression are also popular. Many, when they are first starting out, opt for multi-effects pedals that offer a wide range of options both to experiment with

sounds they may not be familiar with, and to see if there's a specific effect that takes their fancy. Effects pedals can also be connected together should a number of different sounds suit the direction you're heading in, giving you more control over how intense certain effects are. There's plenty to take into consideration before using a pedal, particularly whether the amp you're using is suited to the one you've got your eye on, but it's best to leave it until you have a fairly good understanding of the guitar, and not to get too distracted by advanced techniques.

> *"Any pedal will need to be used in conjunction with numerous other pieces of kit"*

Distortion
Recommended:
Boss Distortion DS-1

One of the most popular and common forms of distortion, the Boss DS-1 pedal will allow you to push the tone and level of your distortion with much more depth and precision. Distortion itself is created through your amp or pedal, compressing the guitar's sound and adding an overtone in order to produce a fuzzier sound that the majority of rock acts use. Depending on your setup, you can layer merely a small amount over your clean sound, or push the gain further to get a meatier, deeper tone.

Reverb
Recommended:
Electro Harmonix Holy Grail

Officially speaking, reverb exists to produce a sound that, shockingly, reverberates once it's been played. In layman terms, however, it's the replication of sound waves bouncing off objects, meaning the final product gains a sense of space. As well as giving your guitar tone that extra depth and layer, it's a technique often used by vocalists to give an extra boost to their voice.

Delay
Recommended:
Behringer VD400 Vintage Delay

As the name suggests, delay is an audio effect that records a note you play before replaying it back after a specific period. The pedal you use to create this will allow you to choose how long the pause between notes is, or the delay if you will, giving you the option to produce almost an echo. More complex pedals can play around with delay further, some even going as far as to make a song sound like it's been doubletracked.

Overdrive
Recommended:
Boss SD-1 Overdrive

There's not much difference between an overdrive and distortion pedal, but finding different sounds you like and linking them together could produce a tone you're far happier with. Where the overdrive sound comes into its own, though, is with its more bluesy sound, which is achieved by being a bit hesitant with the gain settings. The result is a tone that's far cleaner and mellower than the often-harsh and 'dirty' distortion growl.

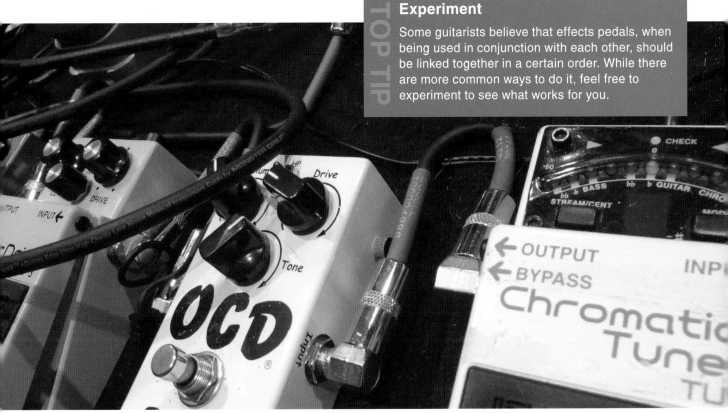

Experiment

Some guitarists believe that effects pedals, when being used in conjunction with each other, should be linked together in a certain order. While there are more common ways to do it, feel free to experiment to see what works for you.

Chorus
Recommended:
Boss CH-1 Super Chorus

As the name suggests, delay is an audio effect that records a note you play before replaying it back after a specific period. The pedal you use to create this will allow you to choose how long the pause between notes is, or the delay if you will, giving you the option to produce almost an echo. More complex pedals can play around with delay further, some even going as far as to make a song sound like it's been doubletracked.

Compression
Recommended:
Marshall ED1

Officially speaking, reverb exists to produce a sound that, shockingly, reverberates once it's been played. In layman terms, however, it's the replication of sound waves bouncing off objects, meaning the final product gains a sense of space. As well as giving your guitar tone that extra depth and layer, it's a technique often used by vocalists to give an extra boost to their voice.

Wah
Recommended:
Jim Dunlop GCB95 Crybaby

A staple of nearly every lead guitarist's setup, the wah wah pedal actually alters the sound of a guitar note to make it sound like someone is saying the word 'wah'. Although the technical side stems from base sweeping to treble and back again, it ultimately exists to add an extra something to many solos. That 'extra something' may be a shot of funk or an extra edge to a lead line that sounds a little weak.

Envelope Filter
Recommended:
Ashdown Dr. Green Doctors Note

If you're looking to add a funky auto-wah sound to your guitar playing, then this cool-looking pedal brings funk back to the forefront of musical technology. Using the simple rotary controls, you can dial in and set your oscillating frequencies quickly and easily, and then marvel at the funky sounds as they then pour out from your amp as you pluck the strings of your guitar.

Get the right guitar sound

Getting the right tone for a style of music is simply a case of choosing the right settings, and we show you how…

> "The introduction of the electric guitar and amplification added a new dimension to the already established genres"

Guitars and amps have always come in a multitude of combinations and different guises. It's easy to get a guitar and amplifier, but choosing the right combination for international stardom is not as simple as picking the first thing you see. There are myriad guitar manufacturers and a multitude of amp manufacturers. Rock 'n' roll brought the guitar and amp to the fore, but amplified guitars had been around long before Elvis hit it big.

The blues, jazz and classical guitar were all around before the electric guitar made its debut back in the early Thirties. All used a version of the acoustic guitar to create the distinct and different styles associated with each genre. The introduction of the electric guitar and amplification added a new dimension to the already

established genres and was about to create a whole new selection of musical genres for the masses.

The Fifties saw rock 'n' roll hit the headlines, typified by the semi-acoustic and clean guitar sounds. As rock 'n' roll evolved, distortion (turning up the amp) suddenly introduced rock music to the world. The late Sixties saw Jimi Hendrix, The Stooges and the band credited with inventing heavy metal, Blue Cheer. Their cover of 'Summertime Blues' is cited as the first heavy metal song. The Seventies saw the gain turned up as rock legends Led Zeppelin mixed the genres with blues and rock, while in 1976 a raw and raucous version of rock appeared in the shape of punk. As punk evolved, distortion and overdrive were still king, and new tones and versions of all the genres appeared and will keep evolving.

Rock
Create a classic rock sound

The term 'rock' covers a vast array of guitar-based bands, from classic rock bands such as Led Zeppelin and Black Sabbath to more modern adversaries such as Oasis and U2.

The term is very much a subjective sound and can be applied to a broad range of bands, but in general it is the classic bands that define the sound.

A generic rock sound is achieved typically with a solid body guitar and a classic amp such as Marshall or Fender. Jimmy Page was a big fan of the Les Paul (as are many rock guitarists), its solid body giving plenty of low-end bass and plenty of sustain and beef to create a classic rock sound. The Les Paul typically offers three sets of double pickups, which helps give a wide range of sounds.

Amp selection to create this sound is a little different. Jimmy Page liked to use the classic Marshall stack, but this was often combined with Orange and Fender. These typically include in-built overdrive to create the distortion needed for a rock sound, or an overdrive pedal that can be added to give more flexibility.

Setting up an amp
Turn up the gain and bass for a heavy sound

Treble
The Treble button should be set to a mid-point to create an even tone, making sure that the full spectrum of the guitar can be heard. For a more lead-influenced guitar sound, turn up the treble

Middle
The Middle button offers the option to add a little more finesse to the bass/treble range. This should be typically set to the middle, number five or slightly higher/lower to add more treble/bass

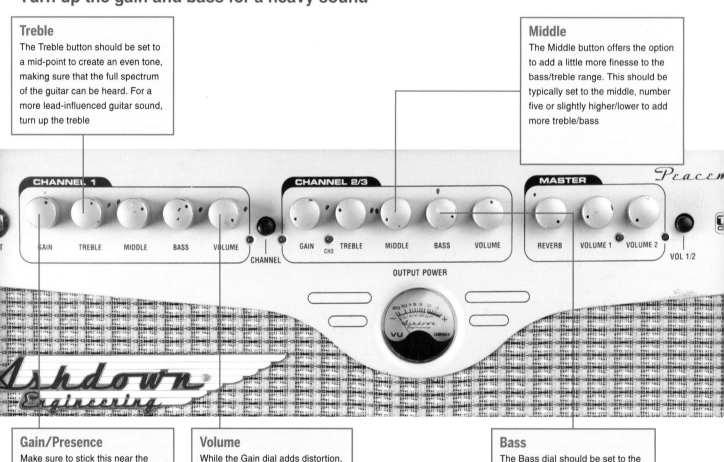

Gain/Presence
Make sure to stick this near the top end of the dial, between nine and ten to create the overdrive/distortion needed to achieve a classic rock sound

Volume
While the Gain dial adds distortion, turning up the volume adds more power and noise and a little extra distortion. Make sure this is at least at number eight

Bass
The Bass dial should be set to the middle as a starting point, number five, to create an even bass sound. This can be tweaked, typically heading higher depending on the selected pick up used on the guitar

Pop
Keep it clean and distortion-free

Pop music is rarely driven by the guitar; it is more the melody and combination of instruments and vocals that create the pop sound. Pop, by its very definition, is constantly evolving, as what is 'popular' is ever changing, but a typical 'pop' guitar sound is relatively clean and distortion-free, though this is not always the case. Classic pop acts such as Michael Jackson and Duran Duran combine both clean guitar sounds and add in a little distortion. More contemporary pop acts such as Take That are rarely guitar-driven. The guitar in such pop acts is part of the overall background sound.

For the reasons already mentioned, the tone of a pop guitar is fairly generic and could even be described as middle of the road. Pop has such a wide breadth of sound that it is difficult to pin down a classic guitar and amp combo that produces a typically classic pop guitar sound. Pop musicians like to use classic guitars such as the Les Paul and Fender Strat, as these offer plenty of tonal range. Typically, it is the solid body guitar that gets the nod, but semi-acoustics are mellow and natural options. Amps used are typically the classics such as Marshall and Fender, but others such as Vox and HiWatt get a look in.

Setting up an amp
Keep the gain down for a clean, classic pop sound

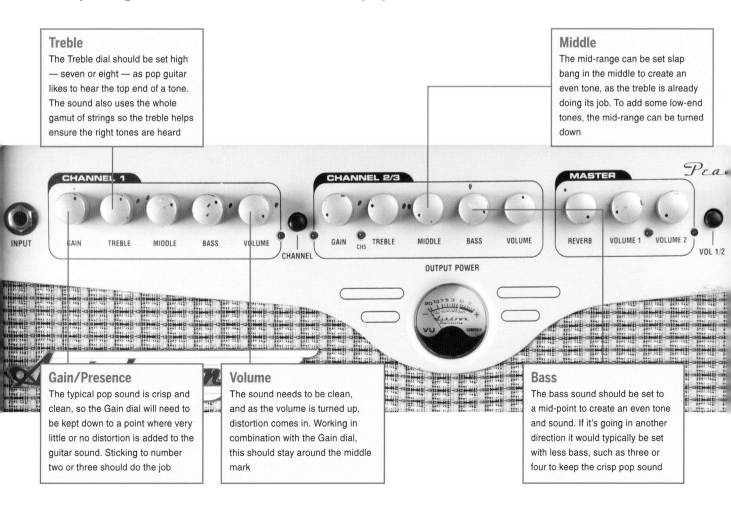

Treble
The Treble dial should be set high — seven or eight — as pop guitar likes to hear the top end of a tone. The sound also uses the whole gamut of strings so the treble helps ensure the right tones are heard

Middle
The mid-range can be set slap bang in the middle to create an even tone, as the treble is already doing its job. To add some low-end tones, the mid-range can be turned down

Gain/Presence
The typical pop sound is crisp and clean, so the Gain dial will need to be kept down to a point where very little or no distortion is added to the guitar sound. Sticking to number two or three should do the job

Volume
The sound needs to be clean, and as the volume is turned up, distortion comes in. Working in combination with the Gain dial, this should stay around the middle mark

Bass
The bass sound should be set to a mid-point to create an even tone and sound. If it's going in another direction it would typically be set with less bass, such as three or four to keep the crisp pop sound

Punk

Never mind the other genres, here's how to sound punk

"Both versions offer a brash, loud, rough mixture of distortion and treble"

Punk, like metal, is effectively a sub-genre of rock that has been taken to a different place. Punk is recognised by two different standards, the Sex Pistols being the originators of English punk back in the Seventies, while a more contemporary version of the same genre is American punk which originated with bands like The Ramones. Both versions of the genre offer a brash, loud, rough mixture of distortion and treble — one of the clearer distinctions between rock and punk. It suits punk's anti-establishment mentality that became a cultural phenomenon in the UK.

The classic punk sound of the Sex Pistols is typically heavier than many of its contemporaries, with other punk bands looking for a lighter sound. The Clash, The Buzzcocks and The Stranglers all used a degree of distortion but with a nod towards a more treble-based tone. American punk, which has obviously taken a nod from earlier punk bands, is still all about distortion and treble, sometimes turned up to ten (but if you're feeling a little more musical, probably only number nine). The punk sound is typically more dry than metal and rock. The riffs are usually filled with power chords, and these are often played higher up the fretboard during the middle section.

Guitars across the punk genre are undoubtedly varied, but once again, the Les Paul is popular, as used by Steve Jones of the Sex Pistols, but Fender Strat, Fender Telecaster and a host of cheap copies help create a distinctive and unique sound.

The choice of amp for punk is again varied, with 'cheap' fitting the punk ethic. As such, Sound City, Peavey and Fender are some of the more popular choices.

Setting up an amp
Use plenty of distortion and treble for punk

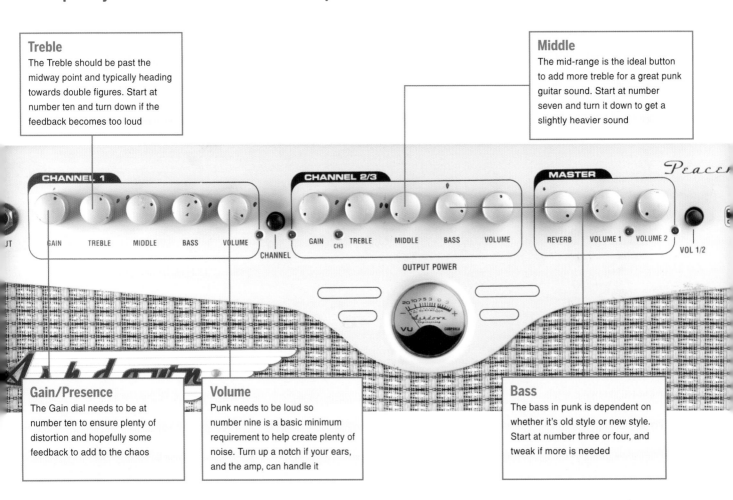

Treble
The Treble should be past the midway point and typically heading towards double figures. Start at number ten and turn down if the feedback becomes too loud

Middle
The mid-range is the ideal button to add more treble for a great punk guitar sound. Start at number seven and turn it down to get a slightly heavier sound

Gain/Presence
The Gain dial needs to be at number ten to ensure plenty of distortion and hopefully some feedback to add to the chaos

Volume
Punk needs to be loud so number nine is a basic minimum requirement to help create plenty of noise. Turn up a notch if your ears, and the amp, can handle it

Bass
The bass in punk is dependent on whether it's old style or new style. Start at number three or four, and tweak if more is needed

Metal
Turn on the overdrive

The term metal immediately brings to mind Metallica, a band that helped define the modern version of metal. But, like all music genres, metal has a very wide breadth of sound. However, there is one trait that epitomises all metal bands and that is the love of the overdrive or distortion. Another favourite element of metal is the guitar solo and use of the whammy bar. This typifies metal guitar solos, allowing for variation on a note quickly. At the same time, metal likes to produce heavy riffs that burst into the high-pitched squeal of a guitar solo before heading back into a dark riff-laden verse.

Defining the metal sound or tone is very much high-end. Guitars need to have the Gain dial turned up to produce plenty of distortion, but there is also the need to turn up the Treble and Bass to help create the iconic metal sound. Turning the Treble up to its top end gives that typical bite to a tone that comes to the fore, especially when a guitar solo joins in. However, to create the heavy tones, the bass needs to be turned up as well. In essence, turning everything up is a good mantra for a achieving a great metal guitar sound.

To achieve the metal sound, solid body guitars are the weapon of choice. Again, the Gibson Les Paul is a favourite, but so is the slightly grander Epiphone Flying V. Another popular favourite is Jackson guitars, which are superb-sounding instruments that have a great metal design aesthetic. The classic Marshall is still extremely popular as the amp choice for metal, but lesser-known brands such as Hayden shine too.

Setting up an amp
Turn it all up to create poise and noise

Treble
This should be near the top of the dial, so those distinctive high-pitched guitar solos offer enough ear-piercing power

Middle
The mid-range option is very much a matter of personal choice, but sticking with the metal ethos, turn it up to nine or ten to help create a heavy, great-for-riffs sound. Try the other way for a really piercing solo sound

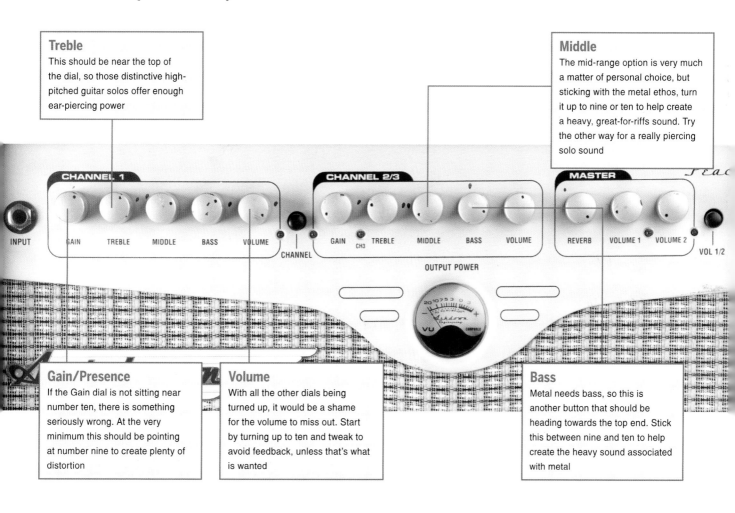

Gain/Presence
If the Gain dial is not sitting near number ten, there is something seriously wrong. At the very minimum this should be pointing at number nine to create plenty of distortion

Volume
With all the other dials being turned up, it would be a shame for the volume to miss out. Start by turning up to ten and tweak to avoid feedback, unless that's what is wanted

Bass
Metal needs bass, so this is another button that should be heading towards the top end. Stick this between nine and ten to help create the heavy sound associated with metal

Blues
Even guitarists get the blues sometimes

> ## "The blues is much more of a playing style that guitarists have to love and learn"

The blues was the precursor to rock 'n' roll and is the sound on which all modern variations of rock are based. The scales and chords are still very much found in today's guitar-based sounds. The traditional perception of the blues is John Lee Hooker in the deep southern states of the US with an acoustic or a semi-acoustic guitar belting some killer riffs and solos. The blues has evolved from these roots, to which a whole host of guitar legends owe a great debt of gratitude. "The blues" has come to connote a general melancholy feeling that reflects its origins and it can still be felt today.

To really appreciate the blues sound and style you need to take a look at the exponents of the art and dissect how they have come to create their sound. There is a long list of guitarists who have helped define the blues who need to be studied and listened to, including

Jeff Beck, Jimi Hendrix, Eric Clapton, Jimmy Page, Billy Gibbons, Dickey Betts, Duane Allman, David Gilmour, Keith Richards and Mark Knopfler to name but a few. It is worth noting that getting the right sound for the blues is more than just setting up your guitar and amp. The blues is much more of a playing style that guitarists have to love and learn. It is a relationship between touch and tone. However, starting off with the right gear is a step in the right direction for beginners.

The Epiphone BB King is a semi acoustic popularised by its namesake. Other notable guitars include the Les Paul and Fender Stratocaster, while it's the classic Marshall stack along with Fender, Eric Clapton's EC series, for your amp needs.

Setting up an amp
Keep it clean with plenty of bass for the blues

Treble
The treble tone is not such a dominant force in the blues, so keep its dial reasonably low, around number three. Tweak to make sure solos get the attention they deserve

Middle
Midtones follow the same pattern as the bass and treble. The starting point should be similar to the favoured choice, so turn down to number three and tweak

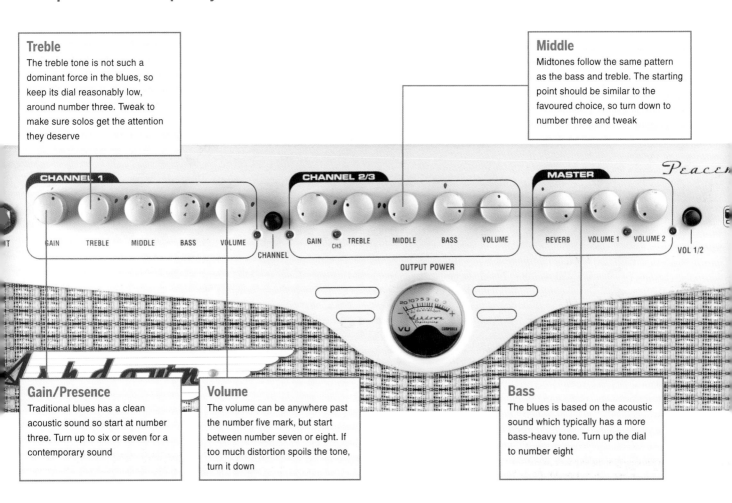

Gain/Presence
Traditional blues has a clean acoustic sound so start at number three. Turn up to six or seven for a contemporary sound

Volume
The volume can be anywhere past the number five mark, but start between number seven or eight. If too much distortion spoils the tone, turn it down

Bass
The blues is based on the acoustic sound which typically has a more bass-heavy tone. Turn up the dial to number eight

Jazz
A real test of a guitarist's ability

Jazz is a long-established musical genre, and the advent of the jazz guitar goes a long way back to the early years of the 20th Century. Traditionally, the jazz guitar was an acoustic instrument, typically a big, wide-body acoustic, but the introduction of the electric guitar added a whole new way of playing. Amplifying the traditional jazz guitar helped evolve and establish a new version of the genre that still exists today.

The style of guitar for jazz has evolved along with the genre, and the ever-versatile Les Paul is often found gracing the hands of a jazz guitarist, but a more typical jazz guitar would be a big, wide-body semi-acoustic, or archtop. This adopts the style of an acoustic guitar with a wide body, which gives an acoustic tone and plenty of body to the guitar sound. An archtop typically boasts a couple of

violin style 'f-holes', which help recreate the classic acoustic sound. Their addition to the body of an archtop helps project the sound of the guitar more efficiently and effectively. They also use a floating bridge, which enables the bridge to be moved to help create a more unique sound.

There are plenty of guitars that fit the bill for jazz, but some recommended and popular manufacturers include Epiphone, Washburn, Hofner and Jay Turser, who all produce great wide-body archtops.

Amps are crucial to creating a jazz vibe. Fender produces a range of brilliant amps including the Fender Jazz King. Other recommended amp builders are Roland and Polytone.

Setting up an amp
A tube amp helps create a smooth and mellow sound

Treble
The treble tones are not as prominent as the bass, but still need to make an appearance. Set the dial to number three and adjust according to which pickups are being used

Middle
The mid-range button helps create the mellow tones associated with jazz guitars, and switching the dial to four or five will help create a smooth tone

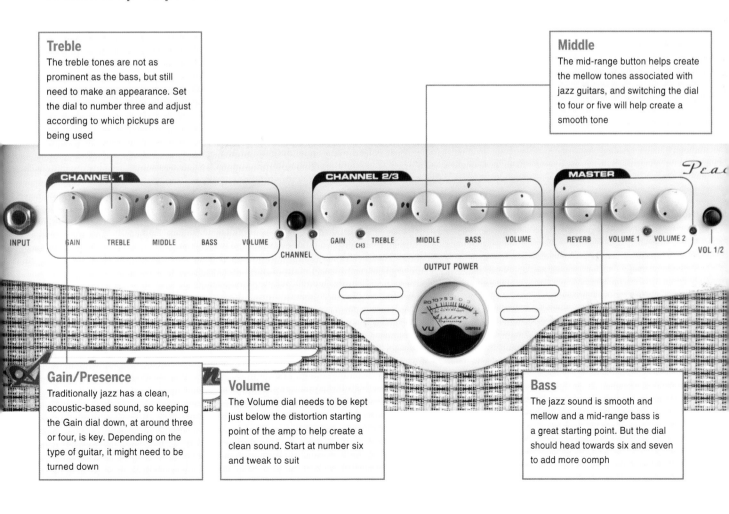

Gain/Presence
Traditionally jazz has a clean, acoustic-based sound, so keeping the Gain dial down, at around three or four, is key. Depending on the type of guitar, it might need to be turned down

Volume
The Volume dial needs to be kept just below the distortion starting point of the amp to help create a clean sound. Start at number six and tweak to suit

Bass
The jazz sound is smooth and mellow and a mid-range bass is a great starting point. But the dial should head towards six and seven to add more oomph

Folk

The sound of folk has been a-changin'

Folk music is a hard-to-pin-down genre due to its origins. A host of different nations and regions produce a sound relevant to its location and culture. However, it is in one of the oldest forms of music where the guitar has a presence and an important one at that. Due to its age, acoustic instruments were the key instruments, the traditions of folk music being around long before the electric guitar and amplifiers. The roots of traditional folk music are still in evidence today, with contemporary folk music simply being an extension of the original.

Traditionally, the acoustic guitar is the mainstay of folk music — rarely is a solid body or even a semi-acoustic seen anywhere near a folk gig. Folk musicians are telling a tale and the guitar plays a part in that storytelling.

With a long history and an acoustic presence, the sound of the folk genre is very much determined by the instrument itself.

There is not a specific acoustic guitar that is a 'folk' guitar, but there are popular choices among folk musicians. Martin guitars are some of the most widely played and respected. These have been adopted by some of the biggest names in folk music, including Woody Guthrie and Bob Dylan. Other brands associated with folk include the popular Gibson and Epiphone. More obscure manufactures are Taylor, Guild and Alvarez.

Alongside these there are Ovation and the well-known Gretsch instruments. Traditionally, folk music is an amp-free experience but there are a couple of amp ranges that folk musicians like to embrace, including the ever-popular Fender and Orange models.

Snapped or broken strings can be common on an acoustic, so always have spares ready.

> "The folk sound is very much determined by the instrument itself"

Setting up an amp
Stay clean and simple for a traditional sound

Treble
Again, the Treble dial must be in tune with the guitar being amplified. Start at number five and tweak to recreate the sound of an acoustic

Middle
The mid-range can add more subtle bass and treble tones. The starting point is once again the middle, with tweaks to match the guitar sound

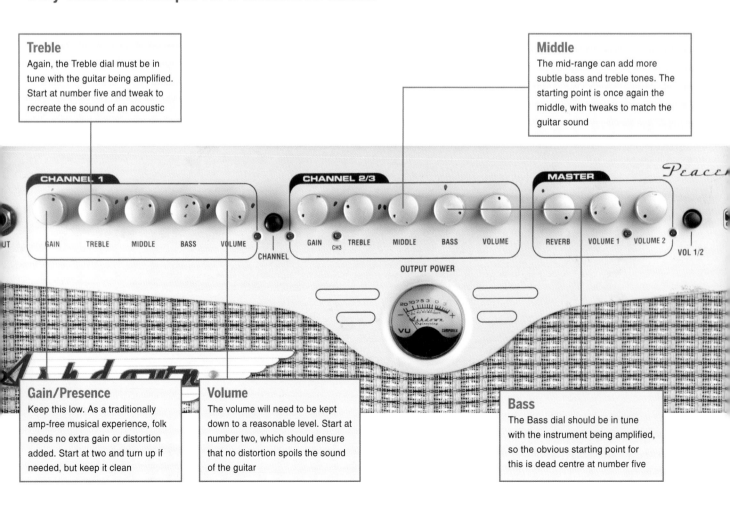

Gain/Presence
Keep this low. As a traditionally amp-free musical experience, folk needs no extra gain or distortion added. Start at two and turn up if needed, but keep it clean

Volume
The volume will need to be kept down to a reasonable level. Start at number two, which should ensure that no distortion spoils the sound of the guitar

Bass
The Bass dial should be in tune with the instrument being amplified, so the obvious starting point for this is dead centre at number five

Classical
Prepare for the classical genre's intricacies

"Classical guitar is one of the most difficult styles to master, taking years of practice"

Classical guitar is also known as Spanish guitar, and has a long musical history. It has been around since the 1800s and is where the basis of the modern-day classical guitar began. The classical guitar is an acoustic instrument that boasts a slightly different shape to the more traditional acoustic guitar. It is smaller and boasts a set of nylon strings, or a set of nylon strings wrapped in metal. It is these combined with the style, build and chosen wood which help give a classical guitar its unique sound. Despite quartets and duets being common in the genre, guitarists are often soloists and need to be picking bass notes and higher-pitched melodies.

The classical guitar is one of the most intense and difficult styles to master, taking years of practice to reach the pinnacle. The classical guitar is as much about the instrument as the

technique and style adopted to create the sound. A classical guitar is generally held on the left leg and is supported by a foot stool. This brings it into a position central to the player's body ready for playing. The typical playing technique is where the thumb and three fingers pluck the strings to create a melody and tune.

There are a host of classical guitar makers, many of which are specialist. These include Manuel Rodriguez, Jose Ramirez and Herman Hauser, who hand-build classical guitars using a selection of the finest woods such as spruce and cedar. A better-known and more accessible brand of classical guitar is made by Yamaha. Electric pickups are used to amplify a classical guitar, and high-end amp manufacturer Trace Elliot produces a range of amps especially for acoustic instruments.

Setting up an amp
An acoustic amp creates the perfect tone

Gain/Presence
The Gain dial on a specialist acoustic amp can be turned up to around number six. On a more traditional amp, the gain needs to be kept down to ensure no distortion or feedback

Lo-Trim
The Lo-Trim is an extended bass button and should be set at the middle point. This can be tweaked to give a more rounded bass tone

Hi-Trim
The treble needs to be manipulated to recreate the amplifier's sound and tone. Start at the mid-point and adapt according to testing

Master
The Master button sets the overall volume level and, as long as the other elements are set accordingly, the volume button can be turned up to get plenty of noise

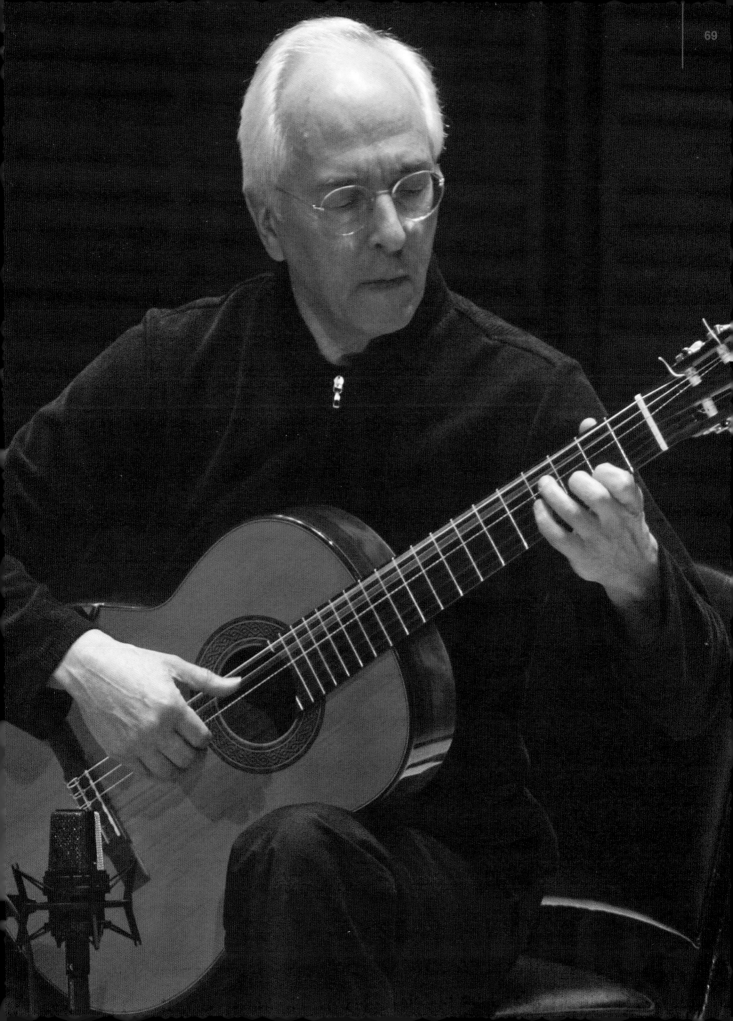

Play through a computer

"You can have world-class amps and pedals at your fingertips for a fraction of the price"

Want to create iconic guitar sounds without taking out a loan for the equipment? Look no further than AmpliTube for your computer

Recording guitar can require a lot of equipment — often more than you think. In a recording or live environment, guitars being played on their own can sound lacklustre and dull, so many guitarists opt to change the overall tone and output sound of their guitars using a combination of pedals, amps and processing. Physically, that's a lot of cables and hardware getting in the way.

Once again, the computer comes to the rescue and presents a portable solution — AmpliTube. AmpliTube combines amps, guitar pedals and effects processing — all in one application available for Windows or Mac. For seasoned guitarists, it's a welcome relief from lugging heavy equipment from gig to gig or studio to studio, but for newcomers, it's a great opportunity to realise the potential of the instrument they are learning to play.

You can have world-class amps and pedals at your fingertips for a fraction of the price of what the real thing would cost in the real world… so there's no need to sweet-talk your better half into letting you splash the cash.

AmpliTube can be used in a recording studio or out on the road at a gig. You can record audio tracks in the app and export them to other music creation apps like Cubase or GarageBand, or simply use it to play guitar with.

Head to www.ikmultimedia.com to find out more and to purchase and download the program. In this tutorial, we're going to start with the basics: playing guitar.

Get started with AmpliTube
Transform your guitar sound

01 Get started
Open up AmpliTube. It offers a guitar effects rig that follows the standard chain commonly used in a recording studio or a live environment. Click on the Stomp A button towards the top of the interface.

02 Stomp it out
Stomp refers to pedals, so we're going to choose a pedal (or three) to transform the sound of your guitar. Select Empty, which will reveal a drop-down menu containing the different pedals available to use.

AmpliTube on your Mac
A guitar player's dream

Import audio files
Click 'Load' to import pre-recorded guitar tracks and/or audio files into AmpliTube and transform how they sound. This isn't limited to guitar either

Metronome
A key requisite of being a guitarist is the ability to keep time. Click the Metronome icon to activate a click to help you stay on beat

Record
You can record your newly transformed guitar in AmpliTube and export it for playback or to use in another application such as GarageBand

Export your sounds
If you choose to record any guitar tracks in AmpliTube, you can export them for use in another application such as GarageBand or Logic Pro

TOP TIP

Use AmpliTube in GarageBand
AmpliTube integrates flawlessly with GarageBand. AmpliTube can be found in GarageBand>Inspector>Real instrument>Edit>Effects. Use it to transform or enhance live instruments.

03 Fire up your amp
You've got a great sounding pedal, but without an amp you won't be able to hear anything. Click on Amp A, which will load a default amp. You can change the Amp by selecting Default>AmpliTube>Amps.

04 Save your sound
Treat it like a real amp by adjusting the dials to change the sound. When you're happy, you can save your sound to be used again. Select Save, give it a name and click OK.

Get to grips with recording

Start recording your very first guitar masterpiece with an Apple Mac, iPhone or iPad

There are many reasons why people want to make recordings of themselves singing or playing a musical instrument, Some people like to use recording as a method of becoming a better musician by playing their recordings back to hear the mistakes they're making, others to remember the songs that they've written. Whatever your recording goals or aspirations, we're here to show you how to take your first steps (or strums) into the world of recording your own guitar playing.

The great thing about technological developments is that there are a number of ways to record music using your Mac or even using your iPhone. Gone are the days of fumbling around in your bag for a notepad and pen to scribble down your musical ideas — just grab your iPhone or iPad and hit Record. The tutorials that follow this one will cover the different methods of recording guitar with different devices.

Realistically, you should open up your Mac if you want to record the next Wonderwall, but if you're just looking to find your feet, look no further than your iPhone or iPad.

When it comes to buying your recording equipment, decide whether recording guitar is just a hobby or a career, and spend less or more money based on these expectations. Don't splash the cash on high-end equipment when you just want to record your rough ideas. We'll take you through some of the equipment solutions available for all levels of recording.

Before you even pick up that guitar, read on for some handy general tips on recording.

> ## "You can have world-class amps and pedals at your fingertips for a fraction of the price"

Top tips for recording guitar

01 Be consistent
For the best recording experience, use the same software. GarageBand is available on Mac and iOS, meaning that you have seamless integration of your projects regardless of where you're working.

02 Make your voice heard
Don't want to carry around any additional equipment? Got an acoustic guitar you want to record? Don't panic, GarageBand has a handy Audio Recorder which utilises your device's built-in mic.

03 Stay in tune
Make sure you're in tune before recording any track. Guitars have a habit of falling out of tune very quickly, so don't let poor tuning ruin an otherwise perfect take.

04 Become a team player
Use GarageBand for Mac to play along with backing tracks. This will not only improve your guitar-playing technique, but will help you get used to playing with a band.

05 Start with a Mac
If you're a new guitarist, gain confidence with GarageBand on Mac before recording guitar with your iPhone or iPad — you can't remove mistakes from tracks after recording with GarageBand for iOS.

Record guitar with a Mac

01 Stay in time
It's important to maintain a steady tempo. Most music-recording software packages for Mac will have a Metronome feature — use this to improve your time-keeping.

02 Multi-take
Recording software such as GarageBand from Apple offers you the ability to record several takes of your guitar playing on a loop, giving you the power to pick your best-sounding take.

03 Keep it clean
Don't worry too much about getting your overall guitar sound right before you begin recording as you can add lots of authentic effects and post-recording processing once you have nailed that difficult guitar solo.

04 Select a location
If you're using your Mac's on-board mic to record acoustic guitar, choose your location carefully. Smaller rooms work best for a clean, interference-free recording, whereas bigger rooms add natural reverb.

05 Crank it up to...
Don't be tempted to crank your guitar up to maximum volume. If your recording input level is too high, it will result in feedback — and a painful-sounding guitar recording.

Record guitar with an iPhone

01 Get connected
Make sure your guitar-recording hardware (you'll need some to connect) has a headphone connection on it, otherwise you'll be playing guitar in silence! A great choice of recording kit is IK Multimedia's iRig adaptor.

02 Save some space
Recording guitar onto your iPhone can take up a large amount of iPhone storage. Make sure to free up some space before you begin recording, otherwise you could end up running out in the middle of your recording.

About	
Applications	22
Capacity	56.7 GB
Available	47.6 GB
Version	7.0.4 (11B554a)
Carrier	Three 15.6

03 Keep your distance
When recording acoustic guitar with your iPhone's built-in mic, ensure you are seated at least 15cm away from the iPhone, otherwise you will end up with a bass-heavy recording.

04 Know your limits
Want to create a polished-sounding recording? Use your iPhone to solely record your guitar then export to software on your Mac, such as AmpliTube or GarageBand and use them to mix your recordings.

05 Use as a toolbox
There are plenty of apps out there that offer handy guitar tools in one app, such as a tuner, chord book and metronome, saving you space in your guitar case!

Record on a Mac
Learn to record rocking guitar licks from the comfort of your Mac with a few simple clicks in GarageBand

Want to hear yourself back or record one of your own creations? Look no further than your Mac computer. GarageBand is a music making and editing application that comes pre-installed on your Mac or MacBook. Whether you're a seasoned musician or someone who just wants to have a go at making some noise, GarageBand is the perfect place to get creative.

Technological developments have come a long way since the days of recording music to tape. Thanks to GarageBand, you no longer need a bank loan to be able to record your own song. You don't even need any fancy external equipment — Macs and GarageBand enable you to plug in your guitar directly into the headphone port and start recording straight away.

GarageBand has the facilities to record any instrument, whether that's via a microphone or plugged straight into your Mac like a guitar. If you don't have an instrument, though, GarageBand has a variety of Software Instruments that sound just like the real thing,

"Macs enable you to plug in your guitar directly into the headphone port and start recording"

whose notes can be typed in using the Musical Typing tool or clicked in using the on-screen instrument.

GarageBand is particularly good at recording guitar because you plug straight into your Mac — it doesn't travel via any other equipment. This means that the audio signal from your guitar, which is recorded and converted into a listenable sound, is as clean as it possibly can be. As a result, you've got a guitar track which can be changed and edited with the built-in effects to sound exactly however you like. Let's take a look at the key buttons and tools in GarageBand so you can start recording today.

Navigating GarageBand
The main features and tools explained

Go back to the start
Rather than spending a few seconds pressing the Rewind button to go back to the beginning of the track, just click the icon to go straight back to the beginning of the recording — no waiting around required

Ready, set, record
Take a deep breath and click the Record button when you're ready to record your guitar track. If you've set a metronome, this will 'click' for four beats before GarageBand starts recording your playing. GarageBand will continue recording until you click the Stop icon or hit the space bar

Learn to play
TOP TIP
If you've only recently picked up a guitar, GarageBand offers video guitar lessons which cover the basics of playing. Head to the 'Learn to Play' section to find out how to play hit songs — taught by the artists who made them famous.

Set the tempo
The Tempo tool is often used to control the overall speed of a recording when using GarageBand's built-in loops. However, it can also be used to control the speed of the Metronome. Click the number and drag the slider upwards to increase the tempo and downwards to decrease it

Time signature
This changes the time signature of a project. See pages 100-101 for more on them

Cycle Region
If you've already recorded a guitar track and want to record something else over the top of a particular section — for example, the chorus — use the Cycle Region tool to select part of the track and repeat it so you don't have to stop and start to get it right

Keeping time
Having an out-of-time recording is disastrous! However, GarageBand comes with a built-in Metronome, meaning you can keep in time at all times. Click the Metronome icon to turn this feature on and off. It will glow blue when it's turned on and remain grey when it's switched off

Add effects
GarageBand's Inspector feature has a multitude of effects that you can apply to your guitar recording. These can drastically change the sound of your guitar recording, whether it's by adding a touch of reverb (echo) or distortion, which turns a clean-sounding acoustic into a beefy electric

Apple Loops
If you want to add some hard-hitting beats or a spot of light accompaniment, make sure you check out the Apple Loops menu. Use the tabs at the top to filter through the thousands of samples and click on one to hear how it sounds. You could make a whole song using just these

Get started with GarageBand
Record your first track straight onto your Mac

GarageBand is a really great recording tool for a beginner guitarist as it's a low-cost option that's incredibly easy to use. It enables you to bring the recording studio into your Mac; all you have to do is show up at your computer with a guitar and a handful of songs, and you're all set to create the next hit record using Apple's superlative music software.

GarageBand is built to record music — whether you want to record just one person with one instrument or a whole band. The software covers all areas of the creative recording process, from initially capturing the recorded sound, to editing and applying effects. You are even able to take a cleanly recorded guitar and make it sound just like it was recorded at Wembley Stadium with just a few simple clicks.

It isn't just a hub for live musicians, though. Even if you have never picked up an instrument or strummed a guitar in your life, GarageBand has something for you. The software has several thousand loops pre-installed; loops are small samples of music that can be pulled together to make a completed song, and there are loops to suit every single style and cover every single instrument imaginable.

Even if you have absolutely no prior recording experience,

> **TOP TIP**
> ### Play it safe
> Recording your guitar as cleanly as possible is recommended as GarageBand has lots of effects that you can play around with and add after you've finished recording. If there is any interference, your effect will be applied to that too.

recording is surprisingly easy for uninitiated with GarageBand. For guitarists in particular, you can just plug in and play with zero complications. All you need to do is connect a jack to a mini-jack cable from your guitar to the headphone port on your Mac (or line-in port if your Mac has two circular ports on the side) and GarageBand is already set for you to record some music.

In this tutorial we will show you how to get started with recording on Apple's fantastic software, including how to set up your very first project, from picking the right settings and preferences to checking the levels and, finally, hitting that record button! So sit back, grab a cup of tea and strike your best rock star pose, and let's learn how to record your first guitar track with GarageBand.

Record your guitar
Create live guitar recordings

01 Get started
Open GarageBand. In the New Project window, select 'Amp Collection'. This creates a project with settings specific to recording guitar. Click Choose, then name the project.

02 Check your settings
Click GarageBand>Preferences. Choose the Audio/MIDI tab. This is where you control the preferences for any external instruments to be recorded, such as guitar or vocals. Select Audio Input>Built-In Input.

Explaining the interface
A look at some of the tools in GarageBand

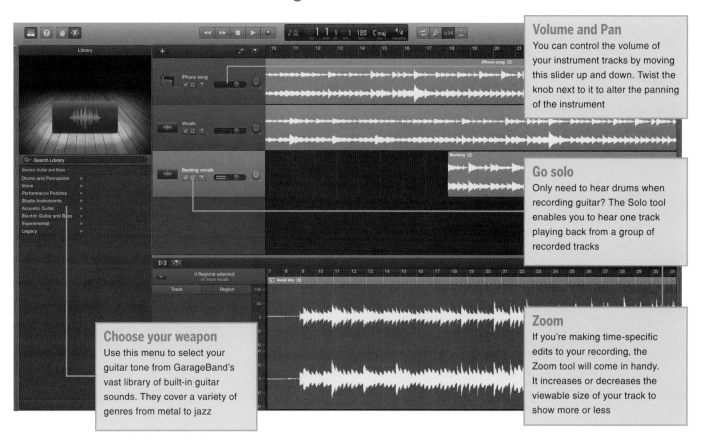

Volume and Pan
You can control the volume of your instrument tracks by moving this slider up and down. Twist the knob next to it to alter the panning of the instrument

Go solo
Only need to hear drums when recording guitar? The Solo tool enables you to hear one track playing back from a group of recorded tracks

Zoom
If you're making time-specific edits to your recording, the Zoom tool will come in handy. It increases or decreases the viewable size of your track to show more or less

Choose your weapon
Use this menu to select your guitar tone from GarageBand's vast library of built-in guitar sounds. They cover a variety of genres from metal to jazz

03 Sound check
Plug in your guitar and give it a strum; the level bars next to the track will flash green. If they glow red at the edge, turn your guitar down using the track volume slider.

04 Hit Record
If you're happy with how your guitar is sounding, this is your big moment! It's your chance to commit your work to 'tape'. Click the Record button and play away. Hit the space bar when you've finished playing.

Record on a PC

Getting a guitar from analogue to digital involves the combination of a computer and the right software. Audacity is a great free option to start recording with

The path from guitar zero to guitar hero can be fraught with obstacles, but thanks to the PC and the right piece of software it can be a far smoother transition than expected. There is no need for the expensive studios or expert producers that come with a recording contract. All that is needed to record multilayered guitar tracks is a computer, a guitar and recording software such as Audacity.

There are a host of software recording packages on the market, ranging from beginner to pro, costing nothing to thousands of pounds. A great option for beginners is Audacity, a powerful, free and open-source audio editor and recorder. The fact that Audacity is free makes it a great starting point for anyone who wants to start recording guitar tracks and more. The program can be used to record live audio (guitar), convert tapes and vinyl into digital recordings, edit Ogg Vorbis, MP3, WAV or AIFF audio files and mix sounds/tracks together.

Recording yourself can be as simple as plugging in a microphone into a sound card and hitting the Record button. Alternatively, an instrument can be plugged directly into a sound card and recorded directly to the computer's hard drive. Any recorded audio can be edited and tweaked until the desired result is achieved.

Audacity is an ideal package for those just starting out, but there are more sophisticated, professional-level audio editors on the market.

A leading industry-standard tool is Cubase (www.steinberg. net), which incorporates enough tools for professional-standard recording. Other contenders include Cakewalk Sonar (www. cakewalk.com) and Avid Pro Tools (www.avid.com).

Using Audacity
The main tools and features

TOP TIP
Hide unwanted toolbars
By default Audacity displays all available toolbars. To hide the toolbars you don't want, go to View>Toolbars and click to hide. Repeat to show a toolbar again or select Reset Toolbars to show all.

Edit
The Edit toolbar offers access to all the typical components found in a set of edit tools. Cut, copy and paste are three key components which can be used to help build tracks. The zoom in/out tool allows for a closer look at an audio track or to show up to 200 hours of audio on a single screen

Take control
The Transport toolbar is used for controlling playback and recording. There is the standard selection with Play, Pause, Stop, Skip and Record buttons. To loop a track, hold down the Shift key when pressing the Play button. Pressing Record always creates a new track. To record on the same track, hold down Shift when pressing the Record button

Audio tracks
As soon as the Record button is pressed, a track will appear with a waveform of the currently recording audio. Users can play back the current track(s). A new track can be added via the Tracks menu, followed by Add New. Click the up arrow on the left of a track to collapse it and allow for the viewing of multiple tracks

Effects menu

The Effect menu comes with a set of built-in effects including Amplify, Bass Boost, Change Pitch, Change Tempo, Compressor, Echo, Leveller, Phaser and Wah-Wah. To apply an effect, first select the part or all of a track and then select the desired effect from the Effects menu

Speed up/slow down

The Transcription toolbar is effectively only one component: a slider. Moving the slider left and right will adjust the speed of playback for the selected track. Move the slider left to slow it down, right to speed up and click the green arrow to play back the track at its new speed

> *"A great option for beginners is Audacity, a powerful, free and open-source audio editor and recorder"*

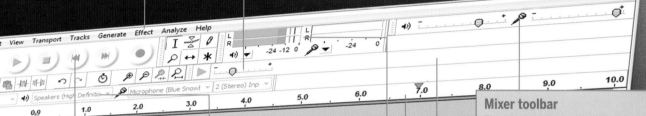

Mixer toolbar

The Mixer toolbar helps control the output and input levels of the audio devices currently selected in Device toolbar. There are two sliders, one for the volume of any connected speakers/headphones and one for any connected devices such as a guitar or microphone. Simply move left/right to adjust the volume

Device toolbar

The Device toolbar defines the audio host, input device, output device and number of input channels. The audio host is how Audacity communicates with a playback and recording device — this is MME by default. The Output device is the speakers, while the Input device is the recording option, eg microphone

Arrange toolbars

The toolbars in Audacity are arranged in a default arrangement, but can be moved for a more bespoke version. To move a selected toolbar, grab the edge to the left of the toolbar and drag into the new position and drop into place. The toolbars can be reset to the default position by going to the View>Toolbars>Reset Toolbars

Timeline

The Timeline is displayed above recorded or new tracks and measures the length of a track starting from zero, or the beginning of a track. The arrow at zero can be dragged to make a selection for a close-up view for more intricate editing

The Meter toolbar

The Meter toolbar is one of the more important toolbars in the recording process. The red bars to the right indicate the recording level. This works in combination with the Input Volume Slider to help to define the recording level. The green bars to the left indicate the playback level

Get started with Audacity
Record your first track straight onto your PC

Whether you're wanting to record yourself to hear how your skills are shaping up, or you want to record a riff you've thought up, Audacity is a great, free, cross-platform bit of open-source software to help you record your playing. Go to www.audacityteam.org straight away to research the software a bit and then download the latest version; it's always being upgraded with new features. Audacity can be used to record audio from a variety of sources and edit it — you just need a few select bits of hardware, which you can find more on in our 'Recording hardware' section over the page.

An input and output device needs to be connected to the PC where any recording or editing is to take place. The output device is the component that will allow the user to hear any recorded audio; typically, this comprises headphones or speakers. An input device is the device with which the recording is going to be made. When recording with a guitar there are two common scenarios: direct input or microphone. Direct input is where a guitar is plugged directly into a sound card ready for recording. The alternative is to use a device such as a microphone. Once an input device has been recognised, the desired recording device will need to be selected from the Device toolbar. Alternatively, this can be set up via the Edit menu and Preferences>Devices. This will list the Interface option alongside the Playback and Recording device.

The Meter toolbar will need to be activated to set up the recording levels. Spend a little time playing with the Input Volume Slider to get the best recorded output. Make sure it is not too quiet and make sure it is not too loud. With the levels set, it's time to record. Users are able to play back a single track, or hit Record again in order to create multiple tracks. Then it is time to bring out the producer in you; trimming tracks, adjusting volumes and adding effects to create a complete pro-sounding track. Follow this simple tutorial to take your first steps in recording, including getting connected and testing the levels.

TOP TIP
Add oomph

The recording levels of a guitar may not always be exactly as expected; perhaps not as powerful as desired. To give some extra oomph to an individual track, select the audio and turn up the Gain slider under Mute/Solo.

Record your guitar
Create an audio track

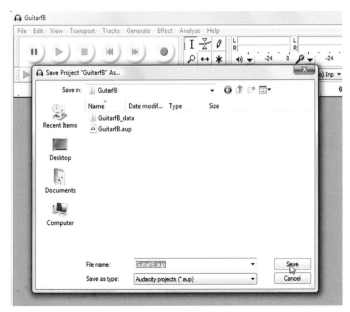

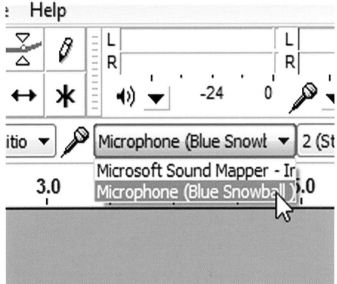

01 Create a new project
By default Audacity will open at a project window. Before you start recording, the project must be saved. Head to the File menu and   select 'Save project as'. Click the OK button, name the project and click Save.

02 Get connected
To record a guitar track, an input device will need to be connected, eg microphone or direct input. The input device will be listed in the Device toolbar; select the desired device from the drop-down list.

Recording hardware
To start recording guitar, there are a few possible hardware combinations to consider

Sound card

A sound card is as essential as a guitar for the recording process. Thankfully, all computers come with a sound card built in. The quality of the card depends on the quality of the computer, but all will allow recording. A decent budget card — try Creative, Asus or M-Audio — is a good investment for better recordings.

Cables and jacks

One of the easiest options for recording an electric guitar via a PC is to plug directly into the latter's sound card. For this, the right cable is needed. There are two options here: a single cable with a 1/4" (6.3mm) plug at one end (for guitar) and a 1/8" (3.5mm) mini-jack at the other, for the sound card (eg http://bit.ly/LynKn1). The alternative is a jack that converts a standard guitar plug into a mini-jack.

Preamp/USB audio interface

A preamp is not an essential piece of equipment, but it can add more finesse and flexibility to a recording. Introducing a preamp/ USB audio interface to the process will allow the user to boost the guitar signal and produce a high output signal. Try M-Audio, Fast Trak or Avid for well-priced options.

Microphone

A microphone is the ideal recording companion, especially for those using an acoustic instrument. There are plenty of options out there, from budget to pro level. A basic desktop microphone will do the job, but the quality will not be as good. For better-quality recordings, a more expensive microphone, such as the Blue Snowball with Audio HD, can be used.

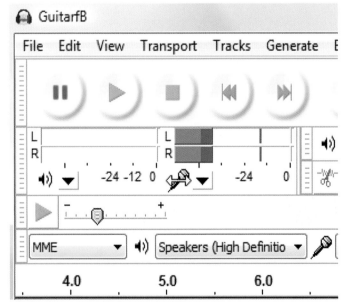

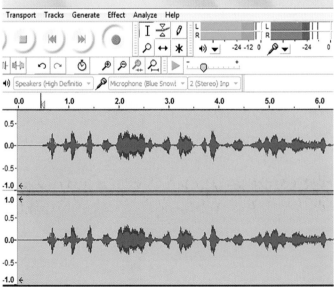

03 Test the levels

Before recording, the levels need to be tested. In the Meter toolbar click the microphone icon to activate the input meter. Now play the connected guitar to view levels. Adjust the Input Volume Slider accordingly.

04 Record track

To start recording, simply hit the red Record button and start playing. When finished, hit the Stop button. To play back the recording, hit the Play button. Click on the track to start at a different point.

Record on a smartphone or tablet

Whether you're looking to record some keepsakes or a hit song, make sure you're never too far from the recording studio with GarageBand for iOS

Picture a recording studio. It's big and expensive, isn't it? Not any more. Thanks to Apple, you can carry a recording studio in your bag or even your pocket with GarageBand for iOS. Whether you're an iPad or iPhone user, you can set about recording your very own hit songs with little equipment required.

You don't have to be a guitar maestro to use GarageBand for iOS — it's designed with professionals and novices in mind, so don't worry if you've not mastered Slash's finger-licking playing style yet.

GarageBand is a fantastic solution for anyone looking to record their music but with a limited budget. The app can yield professional-sounding results with a little bit of practice. For those used to playing in a professional recording studio, it's a great digital notebook for your ideas when you're on the move and it takes just seconds for you to set up and start recording.

The added bonus of using GarageBand for iOS is that it seamlessly integrates with the Mac version of the app, meaning you can easily transfer your ongoing projects between devices with iCloud. Your project will be up-to-date wherever you open it.

If you don't want to record just guitar, GarageBand has plenty of on-board software instruments that you can 'play' in using your fingers, giving your recording a true band feel.

So get comfortable in your armchair with your iPhone or iPad and let's learn how to kick-start your recording career.

GarageBand overview
Get to grips with the features of GarageBand

> *"With a smartphone or tablet you can carry the recording studio around in your pocket"*

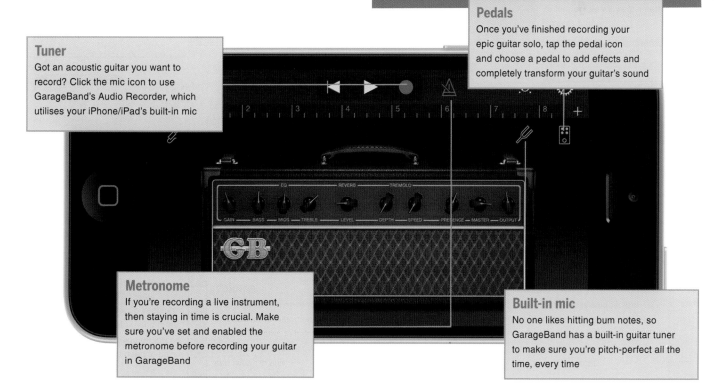

Tuner
Got an acoustic guitar you want to record? Click the mic icon to use GarageBand's Audio Recorder, which utilises your iPhone/iPad's built-in mic

Pedals
Once you've finished recording your epic guitar solo, tap the pedal icon and choose a pedal to add effects and completely transform your guitar's sound

Metronome
If you're recording a live instrument, then staying in time is crucial. Make sure you've set and enabled the metronome before recording your guitar in GarageBand

Built-in mic
No one likes hitting bum notes, so GarageBand has a built-in guitar tuner to make sure you're pitch-perfect all the time, every time

Record guitar with iOS GarageBand
Record on an iPhone or iPad

Amplify that sound!
GarageBand has several built-in amplifiers, catering for all styles and sounds of guitar. Simply swipe left and right in the main interface to change the type of amp.

01 Plug in
Plug your guitar into your interface, which should then be plugged into the headphone jack of your iPhone or iPad. Plug headphones into the interface as well, otherwise you won't be able to hear anything!

02 Get started
Launch GarageBand. Swipe to the right and tap Guitar Amp. The main interface will open. Click the Input Jack icon. Drag the Input Level slider while strumming your guitar to choose the input volume.

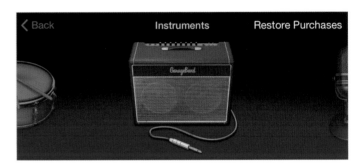

03 Reduce background noise
Toggle the Noise Gate option to On. This will reduce any interference in the signal coming from your guitar into your device, ensuring a clean recording. Tap Done in the right-hand corner of the window.

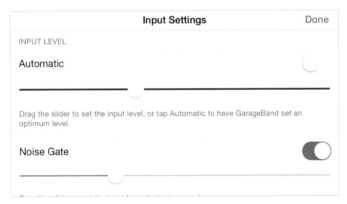

04 Sound check
Tap the cog icon. There are a variety of sliders which change elements of your guitar sound, from volume through to echo. Play around with these until you have a sound that you're happy with.

05 Change song settings
Don't tap Done just yet — tap the Song tab. You can choose whether you want to play along with a Metronome, set a Count-In and choose the Tempo, Key and Time Signature of your recording.

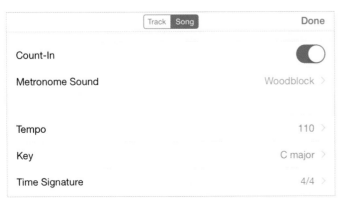

06 Ready, set, record
Let's rock and roll — it's time to record! Breathe deeply and steady your hands. Hit the Record button and give it your best shot… If you get it wrong, you can always start again.

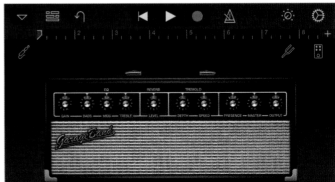

Improve your technique with apps

Give your guitar-learning a boost by using your smartphone or tablet

Taking that step and finally setting out to learn to play guitar is an exciting moment, and something that will quickly become more than a hobby. In that sense you feel the need to consume and learn as much as possible in order to speed up your progress. While there are plenty of textbooks and online guides to help you at times when you can't play the guitar for various reasons, you also have another very powerful tool at your disposal in the form of your smartphone or tablet. Not only can these devices provide you with the necessary reading materials to help you

in the early stages of learning to play, but their interactivity means you can physically practise even without an instrument in sight. The apps over the next few pages are designed to help you at various stages of your development as a guitarist. In the early stages there are apps full of video tutorials to run alongside your own learning process. As you learn and grow in confidence, the apps on offer will start to push you more, but at the same time offer you the chance to be more creative and try out songs you know. With all this help, you'll be the one pulling out the guitar at a party in no time.

> *"Tablets and smartphones provide reading materials to aid learning, but their interactivity means you can physically practise without an instrument in sight"*

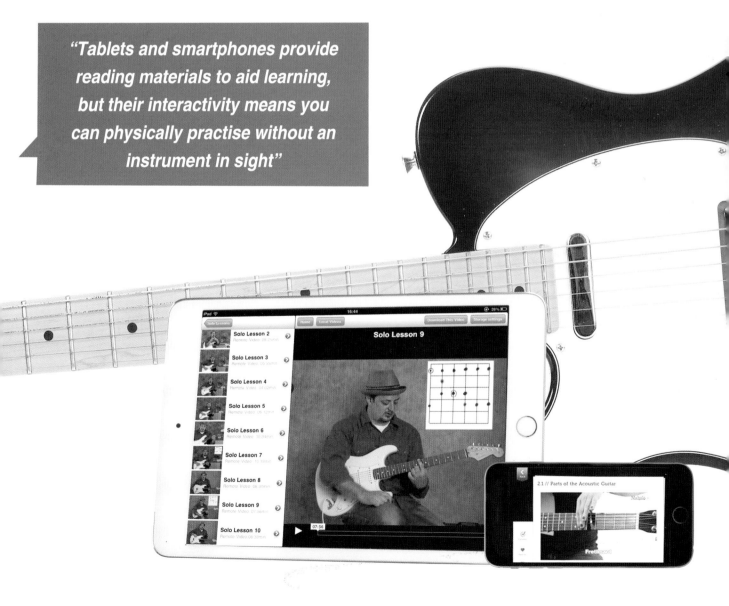

TOP TIP

Go Lite

Before you buy an app to help you play guitar, check if it has a 'Lite' version available first. These apps, which are similar to demo versions, will be free of charge and give you a chance to try out the app before you part with your hard-earned cash.

Top apps for getting started

Picking up that guitar for the first time can be a daunting prospect, especially if it's your first instrument. All the reading material and tips from friends can't fully prepare you for the learning process you're embarking on. Luckily, we now live in such an age that information is always within our grasp, so your smartphone is the perfect extra learning tool for you between lessons, or when you can't have your guitar with you.

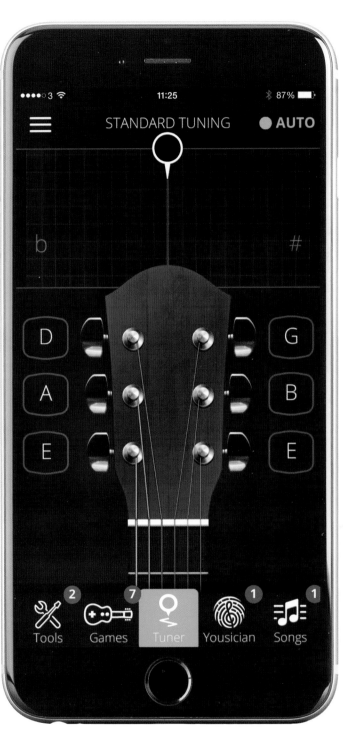

Guitar 101 – Learn to Play the Guitar
iPhone/iPad I iOS 4.0+

As a free download, Guitar 101 is definitely worth a look because of some of the unique lessons on offer from the app. As well as the expected basic chord lessons for beginners, there is a video on playing country music. The app is composed of video tutorials, guides and lessons sourced from YouTube, with various teachers from all over the world. The good thing about this is that the name of the poster is shown, complete with a link, meaning that you are able to seek out more from the author or developer if you particularly like their teaching style.

> *"The interactivity of smartphones and tablets means that you can physically practise without even an instrument in sight"*

Guitar Tuna
iPhone/iPad I iOS 5.0+ I Android I OS 7.0 +

Guitar Tuna from Yousician is the perfect app for budding musicians. This incredibly accurate app will help you tune your guitar, whether you use an electric or acoustic instrument. It works with the built-in microphone of your smartphone or tablet so it actually listens to your instrument while even cancelling out any annoying background noise. There's also a metronome and chord library included, which is quite a wicked bundle for a free app.

Beginner Guitar Songs
iPhone/iPad I iOS 6.1+

Essentially an enormous video library of lessons starting from the absolute beginning, with the first lesson treating the user as if they have never picked up a guitar before, which is ideal for some beginners. The lessons are taken by Marty Schwartz of guitarjamz. com and he starts by introducing the basic chords and trying to ease you towards understanding how to reproduce them on your instrument. There are four main sections to the app, each one with six or more video tutorials to work through. The app also comes with a PDF of a beginner's manual for you to read through. Don't forget to check out the YouTube channel too.

Learn Guitar
iPhone/iPad I iOS 5.0+ I Android I OS 7.0 +

A real basics app taught by Jen Trani, who has found fame through her YouTube channel, Learn Guitar, consists of 27 videos that add up to around an hour-long course. This may not sound a lot, but working through at a steady pace will see you learn the real essentials of playing guitar and even putting your first few chords together to make a song. There are in-lesson diagrams to help you, as well as a progress bar to track you through the course.

Guitar! by Smule
iPhone/iPad I iOS 7.0+

A unique mix of guitar singing and playing, Guitar! by Smule is paired with the developer's Karaoke app so you are able to play your device like a guitar, plucking at the virtual strings in real-time with actual singers all over the world. This might sound quite formidable for a beginner, but you'll find yourself advancing through levels gradually, playing familiar songs such as Amazing Grace and tracks by famous artists such as Elton John, Bruno Mars and many more. Don't feel daunted — give it a go.

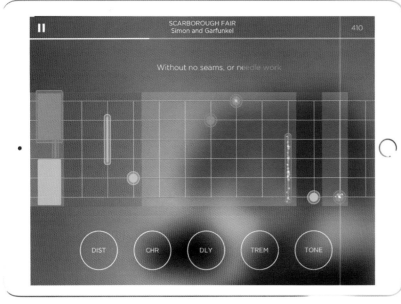

Top apps for mastering the basics

Having found some confidence through the first five apps, it's now time to really master those basics and solidify the foundations of your guitar technique. The apps in this section take a step up and start to look at more advanced features, like developing an ear for notes, as well as improving your general playing ability. Take it to the next level and have a look at some of these apps.

Tabs & Chords by Ultimate Guitar
iPhone/iPad | iOS 10 + | Android | OS 7.0 +

Iit can be a struggle to learn to read music at the same time as learning to play the music. Guitar tabs offer a shortcut, displaying music in a way that is simple to understand. The Ultimate Guitar app is a compendium of over 400,000 tabs on the website of the same name, but with the option to save the info for offline reading on your phone or tablet. The app also includes chord diagrams to help you master the essential aspects of learning to play your guitar..

ChordBank
iPhone/iPad | iOS 10 + |Android | OS 7.0 +

This is an incredibly useful app for learning how to play the guitar, improving your knowledge of chord shapes and enhancing your strumming patterns. A very useful app to have while away from your guitar, through simple diagrams you can learn essential fingering positions for every chord and practice on your phone screen to build up muscle memory. You can also strum the chords to hear how they are supposed to sound and experiment with different strumming patterns to try on your guitar when you are reunited with your instrument. Some of the content requires purchasing in-app, but this is still a great app to help improve your playing.

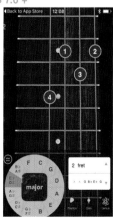

CoachGuitar
iPhone/iPad | iOS 10 + | Android | OS 7.0 +

There's no true substitute for personal guitar lessons but the CoachGuitar app is about as close as you can get on your phone or tablet. Its colourful tab interface makes learning tunes a breeze, and an addictive achievement system provides an added layer of motivation, should you find yourself struggling. CoachGuitar's best feature, however, is its song store. You can browse, purchase and instantly download new songs from a huge online catalogue, ensuring that you'll never run out of new tracks to learn and master.

Amplitube
iPhone | iOS 10 + | Android | OS 7.0 +

Using a iRig GuitarConnect adapter, all you need to do is jack your guitar into your mobile device and you get pretty much any sound you want through any electric guitar. By selecting the right amps and effects pedals, you can make any crummy plank sound like Slash or Gilmore, it's incredible! You can piece together your perfect rigs for achieve any sound you want and you can save your perfect presets to jump straight to the next time you plug in. This is a truly brilliant app.

Guitar Toolkit
iPhone/iPad | iOS 10 +

Arguably the only guitar app that you will ever really need, Guitar Toolkit is absolutely jam-packed with all the essential features you could require. Such features include a metronome that you can have running in the background while you busy yourself using other tools, an incredibly accurate chromatic tuner and a massive library that is full of over 2 million chords, scales and arpeggios. All of these features are arranged in an easy-to-use interface, with a menu of selectable options that is always on the screen. This brilliant app also supports your other stringed instruments, such as bass and ukulele.

Top apps for fine-tuning techniques

Having found your feet with a guitar in hand, you can attempt to be a little more ambitious if you like, trying out licks and other more advanced moves to see if you can handle them. To help you with this, here is a collection of apps that focus on fine-tuning your technique, starting to make your own music based on everything you've learnt up to now and putting it out there for others to hear.

GarageBand
iPhone/iPad | iOS 10 +

Although predominately an editing suite, there is more than enough content in GarageBand to keep the budding guitarist happy. You can practise your chord work for one, and the ability to record means you can keep track of your progress as you go. The guitar section of the app allows you to experiment with different guitar types and try your hand at almost any playing style, as well as the chance to use Smart Guitar and play around with melodies.

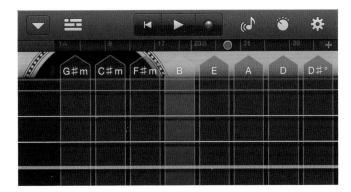

Lick of the Day
iPhone/iPad | iOS 10 +

It does require some in-app purchases to unlock all the features, but this app is still worth a download for the content that's available. Listen and learn classic riffs from the likes of Jimi Hendrix and The Beatles, both of whom have their own collections in the in-app store. For real enthusiasts the subscription fee will be well worth it, with video and notation forms of each riff to help you pick them up.

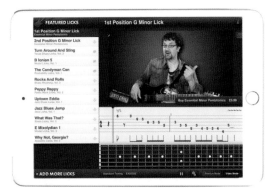

Guitar Suite – Metronome Tuner & Chords Library
iPhone/iPad | iOS 10 +

Jam-packed with a music library of 25,000 chords and 50 scales, Guitar Suite — Metronome Tuner & Chords Library is designed to provide a reference guide for self-taught guitarists looking to learn new skills or fine-tune how they play guitar. The app comes complete with realistic sound effects and a six-string display. Watch and imitate the app to master the structure of playing. A precision chromatic tuner is also included, covering everything from banjos to ukuleles. A great app for both beginners and intermediates.

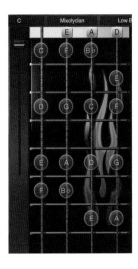

Songsterr Guitar Tabs & Chords
iPhone/iPad | iOS 10 + | Android | OS 7.0 +

This is a great way to try out favourite songs with your newfound skills thanks to the huge song catalogue within the app, hence the hefty price tag (Songsterr is a subscription based app). Songsterr offers tabs for each song so you can watch and play along with current tracks. If you find it a struggle, there are video lessons available to help brush up your technique, but having the incentive of playing songs that you know and love should see you through.

Guitar Jam Tracks
iPhone/iPad | iOS 10 +

This app provides live recorded backing tracks to hone your soloing skills to in five distinct styles, each with seven different keys, both minor and major, with corresponding scale and chord charts. Audiobus enabled, it now includes the added functionality of using backing tracks you've recorded yourself in your favourite music apps such as GarageBand. This app is great for self-taught guitarists needing a level up.

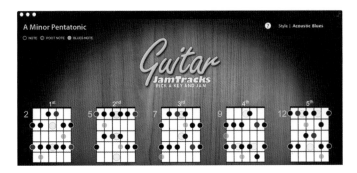

Understanding music

Interpreting guitar tab and musical notation can be daunting at first, but it's worth learning the basics to improve your technique

"Guitar tabs are a system of notation that visually represent strings and frets"

Read guitar tabs

Understand this system of reading tablature and enhance your skills in a matter of minutes

> "Tabs can teach you how to play a complex series of notes quickly"

Guitar tablature (or 'tab' for short) is a system of notation that visually represents the strings and frets of the guitar fretboard. Each note is indicated by a number, which indicates the fret to play, placed on the appropriate string. A basic guitar tab consists of six lines running horizontally and these lines represent the six strings of your guitar, with the thinnest E string at the top and the thickest E string at the bottom.

Numbers are then placed on these lines to represent finger positions on the guitar fretboard. So if you see the number '2' positioned on the A string, then you would have to hold down the fifth string on the second fret and pick the string. If you see a '0' positioned on a string then this would signify that the string should be played open. If you are required to play a chord as part of the tab then the chord notes would be placed in a vertical line upon the horizontal lines to indicate that the marked strings all need to be played simultaneously. The benefits of learning to play guitar tabs are that they can teach you how to play quite a demanding, complex series of notes quickly and easily by simply playing what you see on the page or screen. You can spend time working on the notes you need to play and the fingers you use to hold them down, and then slowly build up your speed.

However, tabs often don't represent how long to hold a note and help you maintain a decent rhythm — so it's best to listen to the actual song for guidance on timing and then practise 'til your fingers bleed! Pick a song that you know really well to start off with, the familiarity should help.

Playing tabs can be as integral to your learning as the chords because being able to pick a lick or solo based on using a tab will instantly build your confidence and give you a greater understanding of where to find specific notes on the fretboard. In this tutorial we

Understanding tabs

By learning how to read guitar tabs you'll be playing famous riffs and licks in minutes!

Although guitar tabs may look initially daunting to every beginner, once you understand what the tabs are showing you, you'll be able to play the notes indicated in no time at all. Trust us. And once you know the sequence of notes that you need to play, you can practise the sequence repeatedly to build up a good speed, smooth transition and fluid rhythm that will soon become muscle memory.

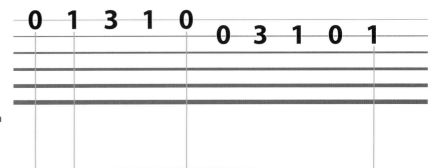

First note
As you can see from the tab here, the first note in the sequence is the first string (high E) played openly, as indicated by the '0' on the top line

Fretting notes
For the second note you would need to fret the first string (high E) on the first fret, as indicated by the '1' on the top line

In sequence
The sequence continues on the first string (high E) at the third fret, then back to the first fret and then the string played openly again before moving to the second string (B)

Take control
Changing strings
Starting with the B string played openly, you would then need to play the note at the third fret, first fret, open, and then the first fret

Read and play tabs
The relationship between strings, notes and chords

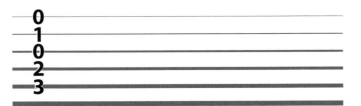

01 The strings
The horizontal lines of a guitar tab represent the six strings of the guitar with the thinnest E string at the top and the thickest E string at the bottom — as if looking down at your fretboard while holding your guitar.

02 The notes
The numbers marked on the strings indicate the finger positions on the guitar fretboard. For example, the number '2' on the A string means you have to press it down at the second fret.

03 Open notes
When you see a '0' marked on a string in the tab sequence, it means that the respective string needs to be played open without you pressing it down on a particular fret.

04 Playing chords
When you are required to play chords as part of the tab, the notes are placed in a vertical line at 90 degrees to the strings. The chord marked here represents a C chord and you would strum five strings in one motion.

Tablature symbols
Here are common symbols that represent the subtler techniques

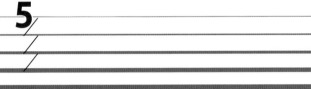

01 Hammer-on
A hammer-on is executed by picking a note and then hammering down with the fretting finger on the second note. The second note isn't picked, it merely echoes the first one. Hammer-ons are represented by an 'h' directly in-between notes, as seen above.

02 Pull-off
A pull-off is essentially the opposite of a hammer-on, so the first note is played again then the fretting hand pulls the finger off the note letting it sound. A pull-off is typically represented by the letter 'p' directly in-between notes, as is shown in the diagram above.

04 Slides
Sliding is a very slick way to move between notes on the fretboard and there are two symbols to look out for in guitar tabs. A '/' between notes indicates that you should slide up to the second note from the first and a '\' signifies a slide down from one note to the other.

05 Vibrato
Playing vibrato involves a constant rhythmic bending of the string, bending it up and down quickly to create a pulsating, wavy note. Vibrato is usually represented by a 'v' or a '~' next to the note you need to manipulate. Again, have a look at the picture above for a more visual clue.

07 String mute
This means that the string should be 'muted' to produce a suppressed tone. The most popular method of doing this is with the palm, where the edge of the palm of the picking hand is placed at the base of the strings. It's much easier to master than it sounds!

08 Tremolo picking
This technique is when a single note is played repeatedly in quick succession by moving the pick up and down rapidly to sustain a melodic line. If picked fast enough, the note sounds constant. This is represented by 'TP' or a series of '/' above or below a note.

Tablature symbols
Here are some symbols you will encounter while reading tabs (n = fret number).

L	Lied note	b	Bend	s	Legato slide	<	Fade in
x	Muted (dead) note	br	Bend release	/	Slide into from below or out of upwards	^	Upstroke
g	Grace note	pb	Pre bend	\	Slide into from above or out of downwards	v	Downstroke
(n)	Ghost note	pbr	Pre bend release			W	Whole note (semibreve)
>	Accentuated note	brb	Bend release bend	~	Vibrato	H	Half note (minim)
NH	Natural harmonic	\n/	Tremolo bar dip	W	Wide vibrato	Q	Quarter note (crotchet)
AH	Artificial harmonic	\n	Tremolo bar dive	tr	Trill	E	8th note (quaver)
TP	Tapped harmonic	-/n	Tremolo bar release up	TP	Tremolo picking	S	16th (semiquaver)
SH	Semi harmonic	/n\	Tremolo bar inverted dip	T	Tapping	T	32nd (demisemiquaver)
PH	Pitch harmonic	/n	Tremolo bar return	S	Slap (bass)	X	64th (hemisemidemiquaver)
h	Hammer-on	-\n	Tremolo bar release down	P	Pop (bass)	.	Note dotted
p	Pull-off	S	Shift slide			I-n-I	n-tuplets

7b   7b   **7r5**   **7r5**

03 The bends

A bend, represented by the letter 'b', is where the fretting hand bends the string to change the pitch and the note is sustained. There are also release bends, represented by 'r'. These are like a bend, but it tells you when to release the bend and go into the next note.

7t   7t   7t

06 Tapping

Tapping is very similar to a hammer-on indeed, but you don't actually strum any notes at all. Just tap the notes on your guitar's fretboard with your fretting hand. Tapping is usually represented by a 't' next to the fret where you conduct the tap.

Tr~~~~

5   5

09 Trills

A trill is actioned when you perform a hammer-on effect and pull-off quickly back and forth between two different notes. Trills are represented on musical tabs by 'Tr' and are usually followed by a vibrato to indicate the full length of the trill.

Applying music to tabs
Understand notes and learn to apply them to tabs

The image here shows the same piece of music in sheet and tab form. It is a simple song that everyone will be familiar with and all of the notes can be found on the first string (E). From the notes on the stave (the five lines on which the notes are written), you'll know how many semi-tones the notes need to increase by and then find them on the fretboard.

Finding notes
The first note of the song is E, so if you apply this to the tab underneath, you'll notice that the first two notes are played on the open E string

Fretting strings
The next note goes up a tone to F#, which is played on the first string at the second fret before returning to the open E string again

High E
The highest note of the piece is an E, which is played on the first string up at the twelfth fret. Check how many semi-tones you have to go up on the scale and then apply it to the fretboard

Dropping notes
The note then goes up to an A, which is played on the first string at the fifth fret before a G#, which is played on the first string at the fourth fret

Give it a try
Practise your guitar tab knowledge

As you will now be aware, reading tabs really isn't difficult, but you have to start with simple pieces of tabbed music and concentrate on playing them proficiently before moving on to more complex pieces with more advanced techniques required. Practise this piece and slowly build up the speed to play it continuously as a melody.

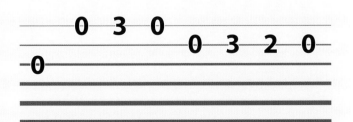

What is musical notation?

Throughout this section we will begin to look at what musical notation is, how to read it and how it affects the way we play a piece

Musical notation is a way composers express to musicians how to play a piece of music through both pitch and rhythm. Music is written on a stave which consists of five lines. Notes can be placed either in the spaces or on the lines themselves, each representing one of

> *"Preceding the musical notes you will find a clef and time signature"*

the seven natural notes in music. Musical notes are separated by vertical lines called bar lines. Preceding the musical notes, you will usually find a clef and time signature, and sometimes you may see either a sharp or flat notation, representing a key signature within a particular piece. Above the stave you will almost always find a tempo marking, either through a number or an expressive term, which will indicate the speed of the piece. Underneath, a composer could add dynamic markings to show the volume they want a particular section of music played. Read our guide on the most common notation below to start understanding musical notes.

Understanding musical notes
Our guide to the most common notation

01 Clef
There are various types of clef that you can use in a piece of music. This one is called the treble clef (or G clef due to its position on the stave). It tells us the pitch of the notes that have been written.

02 Key signature

This will always appear at the beginning of the piece of music. By placing the symbols either in the spaces or lines, it tells us if the notes we should play are flats or sharps. This is A major.

03 Time signature
4
4
At the start of a piece of music you will see two different numbers, one on top of the other. The top number tells you how many beats in a bar there are; the bottom tells you what type of beat it is.

04 Tempo marking
♩=130
There are several ways of indicating the tempo at the beginning of a piece of music. The two most common are via a written word (usually an Italian tempo expression) or, as in this case, by how many crotchet beats per minute there are.

05 Dynamics
p
f
These tell you what volume to play the particular phrase of music at. The two most common are f (forte), which is loud, and p (piano), which means quiet. Adding an m (mezzo) before either of the two symbols means moderately.

06 Notes
The notes in a strip of music are the musical symbols that tell you both the rhythm and pitch of the piece of music you are playing.

07 Staccato
A dot above a note is a staccato marking. This tells us to play the note slightly shorter than we would normally be directed to.

08 Bar line
The bar line divides the notes in to the correct number of beats, as indicated by the time signature. There are several different types, including repeats, which are used at the end of a piece of music.

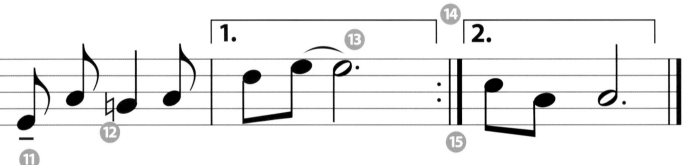

09 Accent
When you see a horizontal arrow above a note, this is known as an accent. Through this symbol we need to emphasise a note slightly more, usually through dynamics, making the sound slightly louder. Not to be confused with crescendo.

10 Crescendo/Decrescendo
Similar in look to an accent, but larger and placed under a piece of music, this is a dynamic marking that tells us either to get louder (as in the example) or quieter (the opposite of the example). The words 'cresc.' or 'decresc.' may be used instead of the notation marks.

11 Tenuto
A single horizontal bold line above or below a type of musical note is a tenuto marking. This explains to us musicians that we should be playing that note to its fullest value.

12 Accidentals
These symbols are placed in front of the note and will indicate a pitch that is not already shown in the key signature. The three most common types are flats ♭, sharps ♯ and naturals ♮.

13 Tie
Two notes of the same pitch can be tied together with this symbol. The second note should not be played again, but must remain heard.

14 First and second time lines
You will find that these symbols for first and second time lines will appear above particular bars during a repeated section where, during a repeat, the piece indicates a different ending.

15 Repeat bars
A double barline with two dots means that you should repeat the music written between the two sets of repeat signs. When it's only a left-facing sign, repeat from the beginning.

Practise and repeat
Learning to read music can be quite challenging at first, but the most important thing is practice and repetition. Through these two basic principles, in time you will be able to play through music without having to think about where the notes are first.

TOP TIP

Read musical notation
A note is the symbol used to determine a musical sound. There are different types, but all are split into two elements: pitch and time

A musical note is represented by a type of dot on the musical stave. This dot can either be filled in or left with a gap in the middle. This will change the length of time that you play the note, for example, four crotchets would be played on the four beats of a bar. Most notes also contain a vertical line known as a stem. Again, this will help to determine how long you hold the note on for, however, the direction of the stem (pointing up or pointing down) makes no difference. Here are the different musical notes and how long they should be played for. You may initially have trouble distinguishing the notes from each other but after steady practise you'll find yourself knowing your crotchets from your quavers.

> **"After steady practice you'll find yourself intuitively knowing your crotchets from your quavers "**

Semibreve or whole note
This is worth 4 beats

Minim or half note
This is worth 2 beats

Crotchet or quarter note
This is worth 1 beat

Quaver or eighth note
This is worth 1/2 a beat

Quavers can also be joined together in either twos or fours. In groups of twos, both notes are worth 1 beat, and in a four, the four notes are worth 2 beats

Understanding notes
Use a simple mnemonic to help you out

In order to name the notes on a treble clef stave, we use the first seven letters of the alphabet: A, B, C, D, E, F, G. There are several ways in which to remember the notes on the stave. If we take the notes on the lines (E, G, B, D, F), we can apply a simple mnemonic (found below) to help you memorise the order. The notes in the spaces of the stave spell out the word 'face', which already rather helpfully rhymes with the word 'space'..

Notes on the lines
Here's the order of the notes on the lines of a treble clef musical stave. If you forget the mnemonic, try to remember that B is Bang in the middle.

Notes in the spaces
The notes in the spaces, as these four show, spell out 'face'. To help you further, try to memorise FACE in the SPACES.

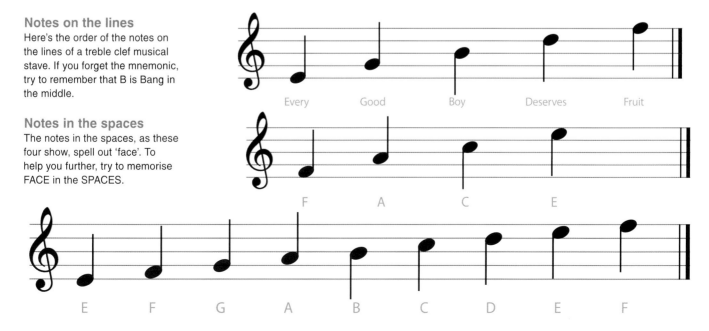

Playing the notes
Now it's time for the exciting bit!

The diagrams below show you all the notes you have learned so far. So, how do you play these on a guitar? Each of the symbols pointing to the notes show the first four frets of a guitar neck. In the following diagrams we will refer to your finger positions through either a coloured or clear circle with a number inside. The coloured circles will always be on a fret from 1 to 4 and these will tell you which finger to use. If it's a clear circle, tat means that it will be an open string. For example, the first E is played on the fourth string, second fret with your middle finger and F is played on the fourth string, third fret. Let's have a go…

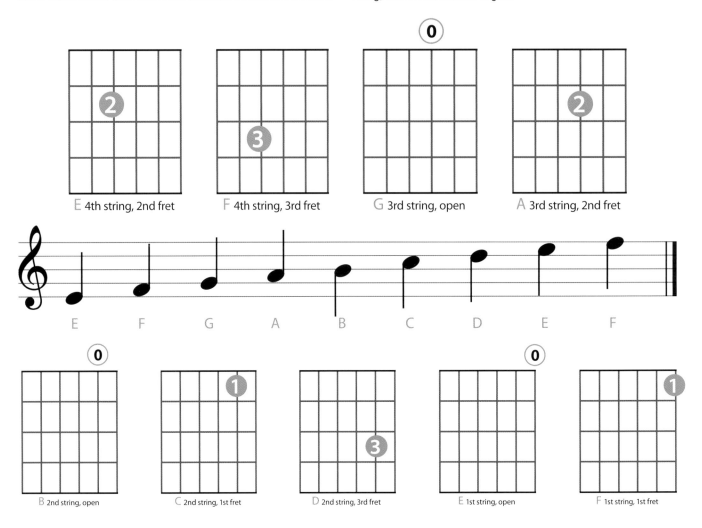

What are chords?
A common phrase, but what is one?

In its simplest form, a chord is two or more harmonic notes played together. The most frequently used chord is a triad, which is three notes played simultaneously.

There are two common types of chord. They are categorised as major (a chord that sounds rather 'happy') and minor (a chord that sounds particularly 'sad'). The most frequently encountered chords are triads, which are chords that consist of three distinct notes. In musical notation a chord is shown by three notes placed on top of each other and they should be played at the same time. To the right you can see an example of a common chord written as a musical note.

Understand time signatures

There are many different ways of changing the beats of the bar through time signatures, and each has its own distinct feel and style

 time signature will always be found at the beginning of a piece of music, directly after the key signature. It is very important as it tells us exactly how to divide the beats of the bar, in turn making it so much easier to read a piece of music. There are two main types of time signature: simple time and compound time. Here's a bit more about them…

> "A time signature is very important as it tells us exactly how to divide the beats of the bar, making it easier to read a piece of music"

Simple time

$\frac{4}{4}$ $\frac{3}{4}$

$\frac{2}{4}$

Simple time is a signature where the main beat is divided into two equal beats. For instance, in $\frac{4}{4}$ time, the main beat is a crotchet/quarter note, and this can be divided in two quavers/eighth notes. The most common forms of simple time signature are $\frac{4}{4}$, $\frac{3}{4}$, and $\frac{2}{4}$.

Compound time

$\frac{6}{8}$

Compound time, much like simple time, is where the main beat can be divided into three beats. The lowest number is most commonly an 8. For example, in $\frac{6}{8}$, where the main beat is a dotted crotchet/quarter note, this can be split into three quavers/eighth notes.

Explaining time signatures

What do the numbers mean and why are they important?

Time signatures comprise two numbers, one on top of the other. The top number will indicate how many beats are in a bar, the bottom will tell you what type of beat it is. The most common numbers found at the bottom of a time signature are 4 (crotchet), 8 (quavers), and 16 (semiquavers).

Number of beats in the bar — Type of beat

The numbers in time can also be replaced by a symbol that looks like a C. This is called common time, but also tells us that there are 4 crotchet beats to a bar.

Simple time

$\frac{2}{4}$ is mainly used for marches and polka music.

$\frac{3}{4}$ when the pulse is 3 crotchet beats to a bar is essentially used for waltzes.

$\frac{4}{4}$ $\mathbf{C}$ or common time (C), is the most widely used of the time signatures and is used in a variety of music, including pop and rock.

Compound time

$\frac{6}{8}$ $\frac{9}{8}$ are most commonly found in various types of folk music.

$\frac{12}{8}$ is quite common in slower blues music and is also used in folk music.

Dots and ties

Understand exactly what is meant by dots and ties

A dot tells you that you should add half the value of the note to its original value. For example, the dotted crotchet (♩.) is 1 + ½ =1½ beats.

A tie tells you to add two note values together. For example, a crotchet plus another crotchet would be two beats and look like this:

♩♩. You would most likely use a tie when you need a note to carry over into the next bar. If a minim doesn't fit in a bar you can tie two crotchets on either side of the bar line. A tie can also offer a 'slurred' note, carrying a smooth change over from one note to the other.

Beats in a bar
If we take $\frac{4}{4}$ as an example, there are several ways in which notes can be used in each bar

01 First bar
In the first bar we have used four crotchets/quarter notes, each worth one beat, to complete the four beats that are needed.

02 Second bar
The second bar uses two minims/half notes, each worth two beats, which will once again total the four that we are after.

03 Third bar
In the third bar, we have used a combination of both crotchets and minims to total the four beats required.

04 Fourth bar
Alternatively, we can fill an entire four-beat bar with a semibreve to get exactly the same effect, as shown below in the fourth bar.

What are rests?
Sometimes in music we need times of silence. These are represented by different symbols called rests

There are several different types of rests. Each rest relates to its note equivalent. This chart shows the most common types.

Type of rest	Note	Length of rest
▬	𝅝	4 beats
▬	𝅗𝅥	2 beats
𝄽	𝅘𝅥	1 beat
𝄾	𝅘𝅥𝅮	1/2 a beat

> *"There are several different types of rests. Each rest relates to its note equivalent"*

How to use rests in music
You know what they look like, but let's use them…

In a piece of music, where the time signature is $\frac{4}{4}$ the rests in the chart to the left can be used in this way:

01 Crotchet rest
Crotchet/quarter rest for one beat.

02 Quaver rest
Quaver/eighth rest for half a beat.

03 Minim rest
Minim/half rest for two beats (note it sits above the line).

04 Semibreve rest
Semibreve/whole rest for one beat (note this rests underneath the line).

Interpret key signatures

Explore the role of key signatures in music, learn why they are needed and how to read them

Key signatures are shown at the beginning of a piece of music and are either a series of sharps or flats. You will see a key signature immediately after the clef in a piece of music, saving the composer from having to add them after each required note. Key signatures explain two things: firstly,

the key the piece is in and, secondly, which of the notes you play as either sharps or flats. The order in which sharps and flats are placed in a key signature will always remain the same. There are two mnemonics we can use to help us remember these orders on a treble clef stave. For sharps we can use:

So, how do we work out a major key from the key signature? If there are no sharps or flats, it's C major. For sharps, you must look at the last one in the signature. If you move it one semitone up it will be the first note and the name of the major key. The example below is D major.

For flats, you have to remember that F major has one flat (B♭). For all other key signatures using two or more flats, the penultimate flat will tell you the name of the major key.

The penultimate flat in this example is a B. This key signature is B♭ major.

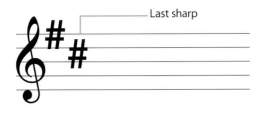
Last sharp

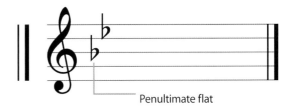
Penultimate flat

Father Charles Goes Down And Ends Battles

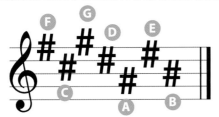

For flats we can use:

Battle Ends And Down Goes Charles' Father

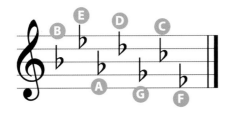

Changing to minor
It's all relative

The sound of the piece of music will tell you if it is a major (happy) of minor (sad) key. You can work out the name of the relative minor key to a major key by looking at the sixth note of the scale. A relative minor will have the same key signature as its major key. This example of C major shows A as the sixth note, so C major's relative minor is A minor.

1st   6th

> *"Key signatures are shown at the beginning of a piece of music"*

Keys
Identifying key signatures

01 Key signatures using sharps
Sometimes you might see a sharp (#) in the key signature. It will be either placed on a line or on a space of the stave. This tells you to raise the note by one semitone.

02 Key signatures using flats
Alternatively there may be a flat (♭) sign at the beginning of the music. Again, this can either be in a line or space, but this time you lower the note by a semitone.

03 Adding naturals into key signatures
You may see a natural sign (♮) in a key signature. This happens most often when a piece of music changes key. This sign cancels either the sharp or flat used in the previous key signature.

04 Using accidentals in a piece of music
Some musical notes may contain either a sharp, flat or natural sign in front of them that may be different from the key signature. This tells you to change that note according to the sign.

Key signatures in action
Here is a recap on what we have learned so far

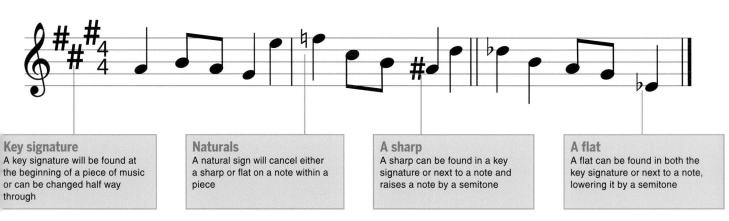

Key signature
A key signature will be found at the beginning of a piece of music or can be changed half way through

Naturals
A natural sign will cancel either a sharp or flat on a note within a piece

A sharp
A sharp can be found in a key signature or next to a note and raises a note by a semitone

A flat
A flat can be found in both the key signature or next to a note, lowering it by a semitone

"A key signature appears immediately after the clef in a piece"

Music glossary

In music there are many different types of symbols that describe how to play and interpret a piece of music

During the course of this rather detailed glossary, we will illustrate and explain a number of symbols and words that help us perform and understand a piece of music. We will also take this opportunity to have a little bit of a recap on just what we have learned in this section so far, as understanding music can be quite daunting. We will also introduce you to some more commonly used symbols that you are quite likely to encounter in a piece of music. You will find a brief description of each symbol and, in most cases, a diagram showing the character in question. As you familiarise yourself with these life will become easier!

First and second time bar
When a repeat requires a different ending, the numbered brackets are used to demonstrate which bars to play first time and which should be played second.

Accidentals
These tell you notes that are different from the key at the opening of the piece of music. The most common are sharps, flats and naturals.

Bar line
This is a line that segments musical notation into a set number of beats, as defined by the start of the music.

Chord
This is where two or more notes are played at the same time.

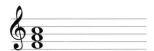

Clef
This is a musical symbol that tells us the pitch of written notes. The two most common versions are the treble and bass.

Coda
This is a sign that leads to a different passage of music that brings a piece to an end. This will usually come after a DS or DC (see below).

Da Capo (DC)
The meaning of these Italian terms is 'from the beginning'. This one is used to repeat a previous part of music and can be applied to save space on a score.

Dal Segno (DS)
This means to repeat a specific section of music that is shown by the above sign.

Dynamics
This tells you how loud or quiet to play a section of music. The two most basic forms are f (forte), meaning loud, and p (piano), meaning quiet.

Key signature
Appears at the beginning of a piece of music and tells you which notes are sharps or flats.

Notes
Symbols that are written on the stave of a piece of music telling you the length and pitch you have to play.

Repeats
These look like two bar lines close together with two dots, and will tell you to repeat a particular section of music.

Rests
Like notes, these are symbols in a piece of music telling you how long a moment of silence is.

Stave
These are the five horizontal lines and four spaces that tell you which notes to play.

Time signature
This happens at the start of a piece of music and specifies how many beats in the bar there are in a piece of music.

Give it a try
Put the basics into practice

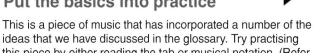

This is a piece of music that has incorporated a number of the ideas that we have discussed in the glossary. Try practising this piece by either reading the tab or musical notation. (Refer to the glossary if you need to.) Have a go at playing along with the track with or without the lead guitar.

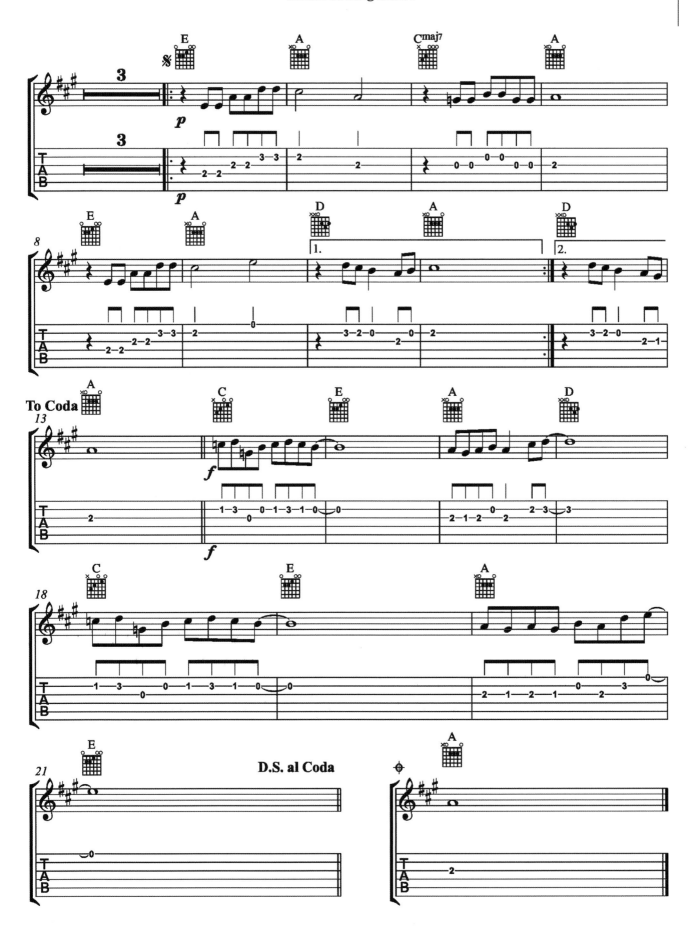

Introducing musical scales

Discover what is meant by a scale and why practising scales can become important to helping you perform music

Scales in music are a series of notes that are arranged into a specific sequence which can be either ascending or descending. They usually start and end on the same musically named note, separated by an octave (the distance between eight musical notes). Scales will follow a set pattern of either semitones (half-steps) or tones (whole steps). The three most common forms of scales are major (a happy sounding scale), minor (a sad sounding scale) and chromatic (a scale whose sound is ambiguous and is made up entirely of semitones). Learning scales on guitar is important for a number of reasons. It will enable you to learn your fretboard quickly, which will become very important when performing music in various keys. They will also help to strengthen your fingers and increase their agility, which will improve your ability to be able to play solo passages.

Your fretting hand

Let's look at where your fingers should be placed...

When learning the guitar, you will often find that the fingers of the fretting hand are referred to with numbers. Each of these numbers are used to visualise where to place your fingers on the fretboard of the guitar. The indicated number will be shown inside a coloured circle. 0 represents an open string.

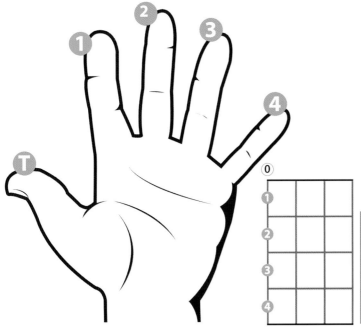

"Visualise where to place your fingers on the fretboard of the guitar"

The circle of fifths

A visual and easy way of remembering the key of a scale is to use the circle of fifths. This circle shows the relationship between the 12 tones of the musical scale. To work out how many sharps (#) or flats (♭) a key signature should have, follow the circle clockwise; major on the outside, minor on the inside. For example, if we look at A major, the key signature would have three sharps (these being F, C and G). The inside part of the circle shows us the relative minor (orange letters); in this case it would be F# minor.

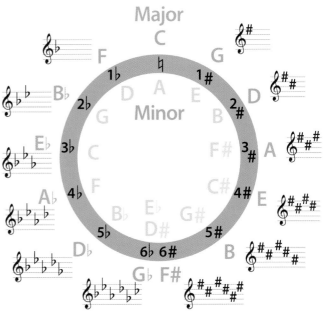

Know the distance

One fret movement on a guitar is the distance of a semitone and the movement between two frets is a tone.

TOP TIP

The major scale

This page will lead you through the major scale, what it should sound like and how to play one

The major scale is one of the most popular scale types. You might also see this referred to as the Ionian scale. This scale produces music that has an essentially 'happy' sound. It comprises a specific sequence of eight notes using tones (whole notes) and semitones (half notes). The major scale will always follow this sequence; from the example of the C major scale you can see the semitones will always fall between the third and fourth notes, and the seventh and eighth notes.

Major scales can be used in a variety of different musical styles, including the ever-popular rock and pop categories. This page will show you exactly how to play a major scale. For this particular example, we're going to be using the A major scale.

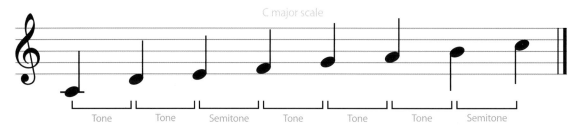

C major scale

Tone   Tone   Semitone   Tone   Tone   Tone   Semitone

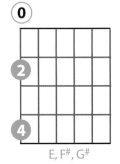

E, F#, G#

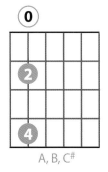

A, B, C#

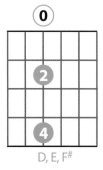

D, E, F#

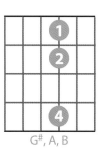

G#, A, B

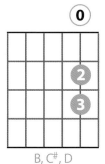

B, C#, D

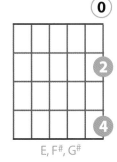

E, F#, G#

01 A major scale sixth string
Play the sixth string open (E), place your middle finger on the second fret (F#), then your ring finger on the fourth fret (G#).

02 A major scale fifth string
Play the fifth string open (A), place your middle finger on the second fret (B) and ring finger on the fourth fret (C#).

03 A major scale fourth string
Play the fourth string open (D), place your middle finger on the second fret (E) and then your ring finger on the fourth fret (F#).

04 A major scale third string
On the third string, place your index finger on fret one (G#), your middle finger on fret two (A) and your ring finger on fret four (B).

05 A major scale second string
Play the second string open (B), your middle finger on the second fret (C#), then put your middle finger on the third fret (D).

06 A major scale first string
Play the first string open (E), place your middle finger on the second fret (F#) and put your ring finger on the fourth fret (G#).

Give it a try
Now it's your turn to try the major scale...

This example demonstrates the complete A major scale. Both tab and standard notation are included. Choose the form you are most comfortable with and try playing along to the audio.

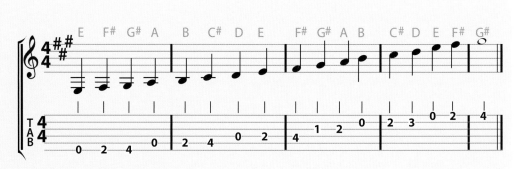

The minor scale

Now we take a look at the minor scale, how it sounds and how it is made up compared to the major scale

There are three different types of minor scales which include the harmonic and melodic, but here we shall be looking at the natural minor scale, or as it can be referred to as the Aeolian Scale. Similar to the major scale, it is made from a series of semitones and tones, but you will see that the placement of these distances is noticeably different. The natural minor scale will always use the following pattern. This time you will see that the semitone falls between the second and third notes, and the fifth and sixth notes. Minor scales can be used in a variety of different musical styles but will create a completely different mood. We will take you through how to play a minor scale, using A minor.

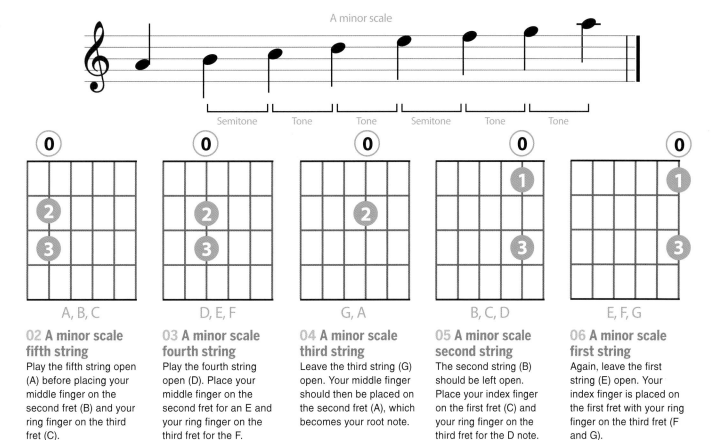

02 A minor scale fifth string
Play the fifth string open (A) before placing your middle finger on the second fret (B) and your ring finger on the third fret (C).

03 A minor scale fourth string
Play the fourth string open (D). Place your middle finger on the second fret for an E and your ring finger on the third fret for the F.

04 A minor scale third string
Leave the third string (G) open. Your middle finger should then be placed on the second fret (A), which becomes your root note.

05 A minor scale second string
The second string (B) should be left open. Place your index finger on the first fret (C) and your ring finger on the third fret for the D note.

06 A minor scale first string
Again, leave the first string (E) open. Your index finger is placed on the first fret with your ring finger on the third fret (F and G).

Give it a try

Make sure you play through the positions carefully

Now try to play the complete scale. Listen to the audio sample and see how it differs from the major scale. Choose the notation you are most comfortable with and try playing along to the audio.

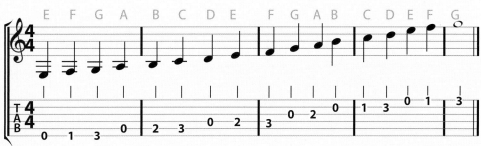

The major pentatonic scale
Found in music all over the world and great for improvising

The pentatonic scale, as the title would suggest, is a scale made up of five notes per octave instead of the usual seven as found in heptatonic scales (such as either the major or minor scale). These scales contain no semitones (half steps) and, as such, can be played in any order without clashing. At first look, the major pentatonic scale can look

like an incomplete major scale. However, this scale is made up of the first five consecutive pitches from the circle of fifths (a musical idea of showing the relationship between the 12 notes of the chromatic scale and their key signatures). By rearranging the pitches to contain themselves within an octave, we end up with the major pentatonic scale.

Starting on C, these notes are a fifth apart

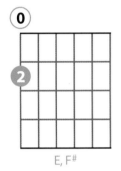
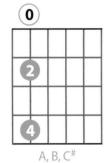
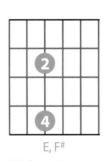
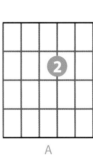
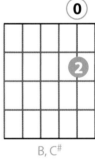
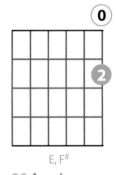

01 A major pentatonic scale sixth string
Play the sixth string open for the E in the scale. For the F#, place your middle finger on the second fret.

02 A major pentatonic scale fifth string
Place your middle finger on the second fret (B) and your little finger on the fourth fret for the C# note.

03 A major pentatonic scale fourth string
Place your middle finger on the second fret of the fourth string (D) and your middle finger on the fourth fret (F#).

04 A major pentatonic scale third string
The only note to be played on the third string is the root note A. Put your middle finger on the second fret.

05 A major pentatonic scale second string
The open string (B) will obviously give you the note B. For the C#, place your middle finger on the second fret.

06 A major pentatonic scale first string
The first note is simple, play the first string (E) open. For the last, place your middle finger on the second fret.

Give it a try
So here is the complete A major scale

As always, practise your finger positions slowly before you attempt to take on the complete scale. Remember that the root of the scale is the A, although with the pentatonic scale this is less important than in major or minor scales. Use the knowledge you've garnered so far and give it a go.

The minor pentatonic scale

Similar to the major pentatonic scale, the minor version is also made up of five notes, although its construction is very different

As mentioned in a previous section, minor scales can exist in various forms; however, the minor pentatonic scale is loosely based upon the natural minor scale. In the instance below, the root note of the minor pentatonic scale is A (the first note), with the rest of the scale being made up of the third, fourth, fifth and seventh notes of the A natural minor scale (ABCDEFG).

Closely compare this minor pentatonic scale to the blues scale across the page and you will notice that they are extremely similar with the exception being the exclusion of the sharpened fourth (or flattened fifth) which in this instance would be an F# (or Gb).

With this in mind, it is reasonable to assume that the minor pentatonic scale is the most commonly used scale in both blues and jazz music, although, like the major equivalent, it can also be effective in several types of folk music and is also found in similar world scales. In this section below, we will show you how to play the A minor pentatonic scale in great detail, and let you have a go at it yourself afterwards. Don't forget to listen to the audio files that are available to download from FileSilo.

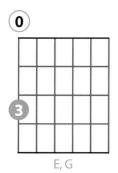

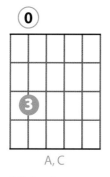

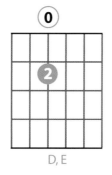

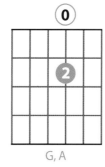

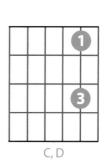

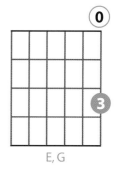

01 A minor pentatonic sixth string
We start with the sixth string (E) open for the note E. Place your ring finger on the third fret for the G.

02 A minor pentatonic fifth string
The root note is the A and it is played open (A). Place your ring finger on the third fret (C) like before.

03 A minor pentatonic fourth string
Leave the fourth string (D) open for the D and then place your middle finger on the second fret for the note E.

04 A minor pentatonic third string
Another open string on the third (G). With the fourth string, place your middle finger on the second fret (A).

05 A minor pentatonic second string
For the C on the second string (B), place your index finger on the first fret then put your ring finger on the third (D).

06 A minor pentatonic first string
The last two notes are E and G. Play the first string open (E). Put your ring finger on the third fret (G).

Give it a try

Are you confident with your finger positions? Let's have a go…

This scale to the right is very similar to the blues scale detailed across the page and will become very familiar to you very quickly. Follow the tab or notation carefully to get the correct notes.

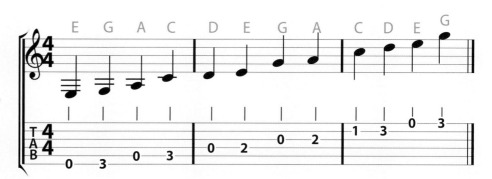

The blues scale

The blues scale is very similar in sound to the minor pentatonic but with some interesting additional notes to give it a distinct sound

This scale is a hexatonic scale (six note) made primarily of the minor pentatonic scale. The difference between the two scales is the use of blue notes, which are notes played at a slightly lower pitch, typically a semitone, than its major equivalent.

Notice that the blue notes used in this example are the C (flattened third), D# (sharpened fourth/flattened fifth), and the G (flattened seventh). The blues scale is often used with the 12-bar

blues chords sequence and blues music in general, although it can also be common in jazz music. It can also be heard in some conventional pop music. We will now show you how you can play the A blues scale that is shown here. Download the audio file from FileSilo and try following along on your guitar.

TOP TIP

Progress gently

This scale is easy to learn once you have mastered the minor pentatonic scale, and a perfect place to start improvising a melody. Over a typical blues chord sequence all of the notes will sound 'right'.

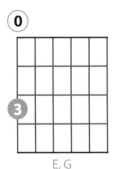

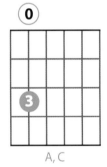

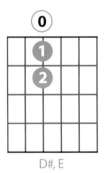

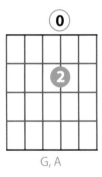

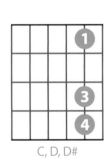

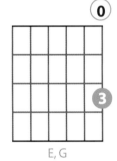

| E, G | A, C | D#, E | G, A | C, D, D# | E, G |

01 A blues scale sixth string
Leave the sixth string open to produce the note E. Your ring finger should be on the third fret for a G.

02 A blues scale fifth string
The root note is A (open fifth string). Again, your ring finger should be placed on the third fret (C).

03 A blues scale fourth string
Play the fourth string open (D), then your index finger should be on the first fret and middle on the second.

04 A blues scale third string
The third string is known as the G string, so play this open. Place your middle finger on the second fret (A).

05 A blues scale second string
Put your index finger on the first fret. Place your ring finger on the third and little finger on the fourth.

06 A blues scale first string
Play the first string open (E). Put your ring finger on the third fret to achieve the G note.

Give it a try

It will sound familiar if you've played through the minor pentatonic scale

As always, play through the scale slowly at first to gain confidence. Pick up your instrument and try out this scale (pictured right) both ascending and descending to improve your technique in preparation for improvising.

Vertical improvisation

Contrary to popular belief, improvising isn't simply a case of making it up on the spot...

These two pages are going to deal with vertical improvisation, but don't let those words freak you out; it's far from rocket science! Vertical improvisation is playing when you choose the notes based on the chords you are playing over.

A mode is another key term, and refers to a sequence of notes that fit into a recognisable pattern depending on how far apart they are. This is unlike scales (covered in the previous pages), which are a sequence of notes that progress at set intervals according to the key. Modes date all the way back to Gregorian chants and Greek traditional music — hence the unusual-sounding names for different modes like Mixolydian and Dorian.

Modes work on melodies instead of the set notes in a key, so modes can often be learned by instinct and a good musical ear rather than off the page. They form melodies that you will most likely find familiar from popular music. Because of this you will often instinctively know which notes and melodies will work over the music you are improvising to without even realising it!

One of the techniques we will look at in these pages is chord wrapping, so make sure you know your chords before you start. This is where you select the notes you play based on the chords you are playing over. So, if you are improvising over a chord sequence of G, F, Am, C, you would start by using just notes that make up a G chord and progress from there.

Vertical victory
Four essential tips to this method

01 Know your chords
If you're going to be improvising based on the chords being played, it stands to reason that a decent knowledge of these figures is going to help. Try to learn variations on the basic chords like minors, sevenths and suspended chords. These are often the best sounding and it's a lot easier to chord wrap if you know all the notes that make up the chord being played.

02 Know your modes
You will often find yourself playing within a mode just by feeling, but learning them is very useful too. The main modes are Ionian (major scale), Dorian, Mixolydian, Phrygian, Aeolian and Locrian. Don't be scared by the Harry Potter-esque names; it's just a reminder that they are based in Greek traditional music. Learn the modes that fit to the chords and which work best with different styles of music.

03 Get that feeling
As mentioned, modes can be learned through feeling alone and you'll often stumble across them without even meaning to. Play along to instrumental music and focus on the spaces you feel are necessary in between the notes you are playing, making a note of what intervals these are. As you develop your ear, you will start to instinctively know how many frets up or down you need to travel to get the note you want.

04 Amp it up
Electric guitars are easier to learn to improvise on as they have thinner strings that are closer together, so there is minimal stress on your hands. This is beneficial as you won't need to focus so heavily on your technique.

"A mode is another key term, and refers to a sequence of notes that fit into a recognisable pattern depending on how far apart they are"

Vertical practice tips
Use these easy methods to help improve your improvising

TOP TIP

Claim it's jazz
This is a bit of a cheat, but if you ever find you've hit a bum note, remember, a friendly note is never more than half a tone away, so bend it up and make out like you intended to play the wrong one all along!

Improvise to other styles
Conversely, try improvising to music you hate. It will open up whole new phrases on the guitar that you may not have found before, and being outside of your comfort zone is a good learning toolFinding notes

Don't look now
If you're feeling especially brave, why not try it blind? It's easy to see the notes you're playing, but when improvising you'll be going on sound, not sight. Try and see where the notes come to you from instinct and sound

Free playing
A strange but good trick is to zone out and play guitar while watching the TV or a film. You'll find that when you're not concentrating, the notes come to you. Almost like free writing, but with music instead of words

Play along
To get a feel for vertical improvising, why not practise to the music you love? It will feel familiar because you know and enjoy it, and you are relaxed in your comfort zone

Try dance music
Dance music may be repetitive, but it's a good way of focusing on improvising over minimal chord changes instead of something more complex

Use effects pedals
Try using effects pedals. Changing the sound of a note changes how you hear it and how it sounds in the context of the music you're playing over

Give it a try
Follow this tab for examples of modes to use while improvising

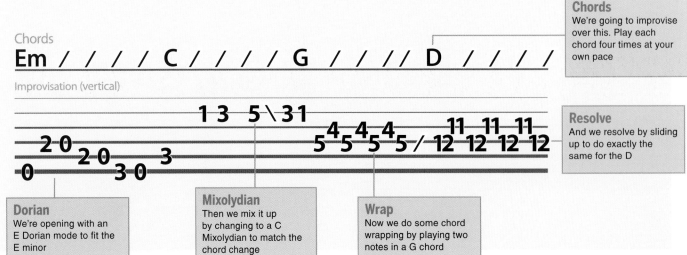

Chords

Em / / / / C / / / / G / / / / D / / / /

Chords
We're going to improvise over this. Play each chord four times at your own pace

Improvisation (vertical)

Resolve
And we resolve by sliding up to do exactly the same for the D

Dorian
We're opening with an E Dorian mode to fit the E minor

Mixolydian
Then we mix it up by changing to a C Mixolydian to match the chord change

Wrap
Now we do some chord wrapping by playing two notes in a G chord

Play in the style of...

Discover how certain genres get that distinct sound and how you can achieve it

"Ultimately, discovering which style suits you will change the setup you have"

Rock

From the Rolling Stones to Queens of the Stone Age, rock is one of the most versatile of genres

Out of every genre, rock may be the most difficult to define. Since its inception in the Forties, it's a term that's used to describe anything from Elvis Presley to — in the modern day — the Foo Fighters. There are, as ever, multiple trends that tie it all together, the electric guitar being one of the many staples. Typically, rock songs follow a 4/4 time signature and are structured around the concept of verse/chorus/repeat.

Ultimately, discovering which style suits you will drastically change the setup you have. Everything from the Fender Stratocaster to a Gibson Les Paul has been hailed as the perfect rock guitar, but both will give you very different tones and drastically shift the direction you are heading in. Your best bet is to see what guitar your favourite band plays, or what guitar takes the lead in your favourite songs and then do your best to follow suit. Take your time to experiment with different models.

Rock essentials

The pieces of kit you need to be a rock star

Epiphone Les Paul Special II
The Gibson Les Paul is one of the finest rock guitars on the planet, and the Epiphone version — which is one of Gibson's subsidiary companies — produces a cheaper model that will serve any beginner.

Ernie Ball Regular Slinky Strings
Ernie Ball's regular slinky set of strings will help the tone of your guitar by giving a compact distorted sound, and allowing the clean tone to ring out as you play like it really needs to for a classic rock sound.

Marshall MG30DFX
As is the case with many amps, there are cheaper options out there, but this Marshall combo will produce both a decent clean and distorted sound as you experiment to find your own tone.

Boss DS-1 Distortion Pedal
For getting more of a gritty sound from your guitar, the Boss DS-1 distortion pedal is simple to use and does its job solidly. It lacks any real warm tones, but works well with most amps.

Guns N' Roses
Take inspiration from rock musicians

Guns N' Roses are an American hard rock band who have been credited with the revival of mainstream popularity of rock music. The original line up included Axl Rose on vocals and Slash on lead guitar. Entirely self taught, Slash would learn to play guitar through listening to music and replicating what he heard. His playing is based on blues licks and Seventies-sounding riffs, and a sound achieved through his preference for the Gibson Les Paul guitar and Marshall Amp. He relies on various scales including the minor pentatonic and blues, with a main feature being his use of double stops, where two notes are played together.

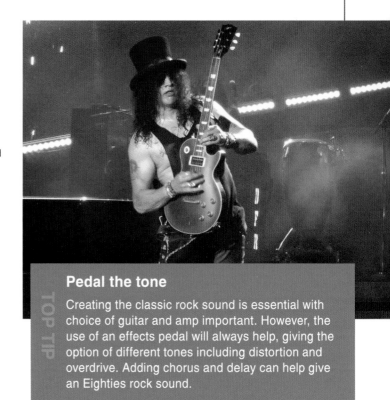

Pedal the tone

Creating the classic rock sound is essential with choice of guitar and amp important. However, the use of an effects pedal will always help, giving the option of different tones including distortion and overdrive. Adding chorus and delay can help give an Eighties rock sound.

Give it a try
Practise the below

Metal
From heavy metal to thrash, there's a lot more to metal than what meets the eye

Metal has changed significantly over the years.

Brought to the forefront by bands like Black Sabbath and then hardened in the Eighties thanks to Metallica, Slayer, Megadeth and Anthrax, the genre is now more fractured than ever before.

A distinct sound has remained true, however, namely a succinct distorted quality backed up with long guitar solos and a thick, deep tone. At its core, the development of metal has come in how much bands have tried to push it. Sludge metal, for example, is almost unrecognisable from thrash, and yet both were born out of the same ideas. Along with this, specific guitars and amps have become synonymous with the genre, with a large portion of players seeking out the likes of Marshall or Mesa Boogie. Take a look at Ibanez RG guitars, Fender Telecasters and the iconic Gibson Flying V - all guitars that have graced metal stages.

Metal essentials
Wig not included

ESP LTD Viper-10
ESP are the go-to make for metal guitarists. Its LTD range offers an accessible way to purchase guitars at a lower price, and this Viper is perfect for those starting out.

Ernie Ball Power Slinky Strings
These top-heavy Ernie Ball power slinky strings will provide your guitar with a deep, powerful tone for producing harder riffs.

Line 6 Uber Metal pedal
Pedals will always be an issue when not run through a stack, but Line 6's Uber Metal pedal will push your distortion beyond a combo amp.

Blackstar ID:60TVP Combo Amplifer
There are cheaper combo amps available, but for capturing that metal-esque sound at a relatively cheap price this is your best bet.

Black Sabbath
Take inspiration from metal musicians

Hailed as the Godfathers of Heavy Metal, they burst onto the scene in the early Seventies, combining Tommy Iommi's heavily distorted riffs and Ozzy Osbourne's occult verse, in a distinctive style that has widely influenced generations of bands and sub-genres that succeeded them.

Their iconic 1970 Paranoid brought them chart-topping success in the UK and spread their fame worldwide. It set the standard by which all others would be judged, including legendary tracks such as War Pigs, Iron Man and the eponymous Paranoid.

Tommy Iommi's individual style combines the use of Gibson SG guitars, blues-infused riffs and a playing style that looks to combine rhythm and lead into one all encompassing role. So turn up the gain and give these riffs a try.

Palm muting

Palm muting is performed by resting the side of your picking hand on the strings close to the bridge when strumming. Done right it should produce the tone of the note but stop ringing out almost immediately. Give it a try now and reproduce that classic metal 'chugg'.

Give it a try
Practise the below

Punk

Punk didn't begin and end with the Sex Pistols. It continued to evolve...

"Punk featured heavily distorted guitars and simple power-chord structures"

P unk rock music developed during the mid Seventies as bands liked the Ramones (in America) and the Sex Pistols (in the UK) captivated crowds with their short, energy-filled and often anti-establishment songs.

Many saw the punk movement as a response to the popular, overblown, ten-minute progressive-rock epics of the time. So instead of grandiose solos and multiple time-signature changes found in many prog songs, punk rock featured heavily distorted guitars, relatively low production values and simple power-chord structures.

Inevitably, this sound evolved over time, and gave rise to numerous sub-genres such as faster and heavier hardcore punk in the early Eighties, and the laid-back skate punk in the early Nineties. However, in the mid to late Nineties, the more radio-friendly pop punk scene developed. While song structures generally remained simplistic, the lyrics were often less abrasive and production was slightly cleaner, although the high-energy, power-chord-filled guitar lines remained as powerful as ever.

If you want to check out a pop-punk album, there aren't many better than The Offspring's Americana. The chugging palm-muted riffs, catchy vocal melodies and fast drumbeats of the California

band's magnum opus are often cited as introducing a whole new generation to the genre.

Punk essentials

Take on the establishment

Thickish pick
You'll need a durable pick for playing punk. The 0.88mm Brain pick from Snarling Dogs is one of the best, in our opinion.

Locking strap
Punk rock is often high-energy, so make sure that your guitar stays secure with a locking strap like this one.

Boss DS-1
Tone isn't incredibly important in punk, but distortion certainly is. Use the Boss DS-1 pedal to get a great distorted sound.

Marshall MG15FX amp
This amp from Marshall contains all you need: a couple of effects and some serious volume.

Ramones
Take inspiration from punk musicians

One of the first punk bands ever, the Ramones were known for their quick, up-tempo, chord-filled songs — especially during the band's early days. The band was a major influence on the punk movement of the Seventies. Their guitarist, the late Johnny Ramone, was known for his simple, distorted chord progressions and fast, down-stroked power chords. True to the genre he helped create, Johnny never really indulged in guitar solos, and those he did play on the Ramones' records were usually kept simple, often imitating melodies heard earlier in the song. Despite the simplicity of his work, Johnny's unique style of playing has deservedly earned him recognition, and he has influenced several key guitarists throughout the world of rock.

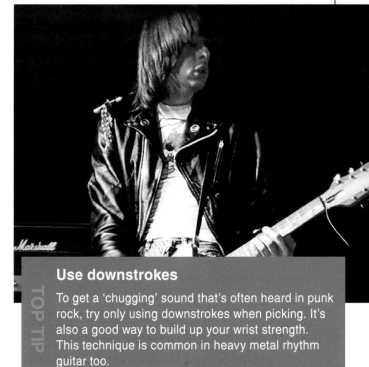

TOP TIP

Use downstrokes

To get a 'chugging' sound that's often heard in punk rock, try only using downstrokes when picking. It's also a good way to build up your wrist strength. This technique is common in heavy metal rhythm guitar too.

Give it a try
Practise the below

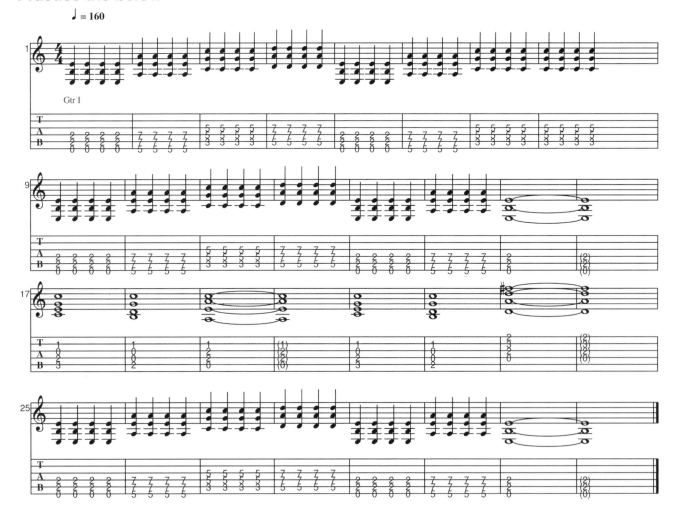

Indie

Indie music is everywhere nowadays, so get to grips with the sound that defined the Nineties

Since its inception in the late-Eighties, indie rock has been a constant in our lives, emerging from both sides of the Atlantic and taking on various forms throughout the years.

From early American alternative-rock and Nineties Britpop to the power chord-loving 'The' bands of the early Noughties and more electronic-heavy bands of recent times, indie has undergone many an evolution over the past 25 years. As such, the indie sound is quite hard to pin down and define. One thing for sure is you know it when you hear it.

Affectionately nicknamed 'indie' as a shorthand for 'independent' (it used to describe the music produced on post-punk labels in the mid-Eighties), the indie genre rejects the refined nature of squeaky-clean mainstream pop and rock. The guitar sound therefore often employs a slight distortion (although many indie bands do utilise a clean tone), as well as playful and irregular chord progressions. Common indie chord types include the minor seventh and major seventh (m7 and maj7 respectively).

These help separate indie rock from the basic power chords of classic rock music. While technical guitar solos aren't especially

common, indie rock does have a lot of lead breaks in which the lead guitarist plays a simple hook or melody over the chords provided by the rhythm.

Indie essentials
Cool kit to help create that indie sound

Multi-effects pedal
Use a multi-FX pedal to utilise the arsenal of effects at your feet. The Zoom G1N is best for those who are on a budget.

Spider amp
Combine a multi-FX pedal with an amp with effects such as the Spider IV 15, and you'll never want for a sound again!

Guitar strap
A strap is essential for any guitarist, so why not try one similar to what Britpop legend Noel Gallagher would have used?

Slim pick
You don't need to be hitting the strings too hard, so use a light pick like a 0.60mm to make things easier for yourself.

Arctic Monkeys
Take inspiration from…

Born out of the MySpace boom, the Arctic Monkeys achieved early success in the post-punk, indie-rock revival of the mid-Noughties with I Bet You Look Good On The Dancefloor and When The Sun Goes Down, managing to reach number one on the charts with little promotion. Their debut album also became the fastest selling debut in UK chart history.

Even during the recent decline in the popularity of indie music, the Arctic Monkeys have stayed relevant by undergoing many stylistic changes through the years. Through it all they have maintained their lyrical flair, catchy riffs and rhythms and the signature driving beats that separated them from the crowd in the early days.

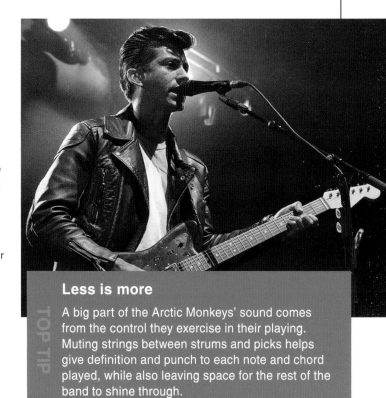

Less is more

A big part of the Arctic Monkeys' sound comes from the control they exercise in their playing. Muting strings between strums and picks helps give definition and punch to each note and chord played, while also leaving space for the rest of the band to shine through.

Give it a try
Practise the below

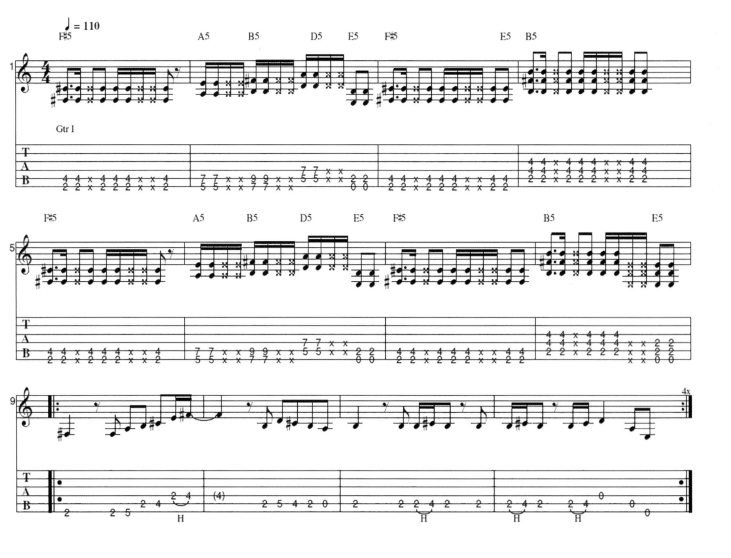

Folk

Characterised by the likes of Bob Dylan, folk music harks back to a more simple time

> *"A folk sound can be achieved with a steel-string acoustic guitar and using your fingers to pick"*

Contemporary folk music is hard to define, but easy to identify.

Although folk music in its purest form has been around long before guitars as we know them even existed, the revival in the mid 20th Century is arguably what is associated with the term 'folk rock'. The genre was pioneered by Los Angeles band The Byrds, who started playing traditional folk music with rock instrumentation and this is when the phrase 'folk rock' was first coined. In the latter part of this revival in the early Sixties, luminaries like Bob Dylan and Simon & Garfunkel produced chart-topping acoustic masterpieces. Although both acts would later incorporate electric elements (with a degree of controversy in Dylan's case), they still retained a folk-rock sound.

Thumb and strum

TOP TIP

Try experimenting with using a thumb pick. This will allow you to easily switch between fingerstyle picking, as well as picking and strumming utilising the pick. This works well for songs that make use of picking during verses, but require greater intensity and fluidity of strumming on choruses.

Folk music is defined by a sound similar to what these artists produced in their early careers, and can be achieved with a steel-string acoustic or semi-acoustic guitar, and by using your fingers to pick (with no plectrum in sight). Often, there is only one guitar playing, and this technique enables guitarists to pick bass notes while playing higher-pitched at the same time — something that is impossible to do when using a plectrum!

Folk essentials
Freewheel with this gear

Steel-string acoustic
With a great sound and coming at a reasonable price, the Fender CF-140S is the perfect folk guitar for beginners.

Clip-on tuner
Staying in tune is absolutely vital. Make sure you're okay with the Korg Pitchclip, which clips to the top of your guitar

Soundhole pickup
The Neo-D soundhole pickup fits inside your guitar and enables you to get more volume from your folk guitar playing.

Spare strings
Snapped and broken strings are incredibly common on acoustic guitars. Get yourself a spare set just in case.

Fairport Convention
Take inspiration from...

Achieving initial success as a British imitation of the San Francisco movement, it wasn't until the inclusion of the inimitable Sandy Denny for their second album that Fairport Convention's folk roots started to take place. Their following albums, Unhalfbricking and the seminal Liege & Lief, would go on to define the folk rock genre and stand as a guide to all those who followed.

Musically, guitarist Richard Thompson conceived a blend of the signature folk and blues fingerpicking of the early acoustic artists with a slightly distorted, mellow guitar tone which can be heard underpinning a track like Who Knows Where The Time Goes?

"Thompson conceived a blend of folk and blues fingerpicking with a slightly distorted, mellow guitar tone"

Give it a try
Practise the below

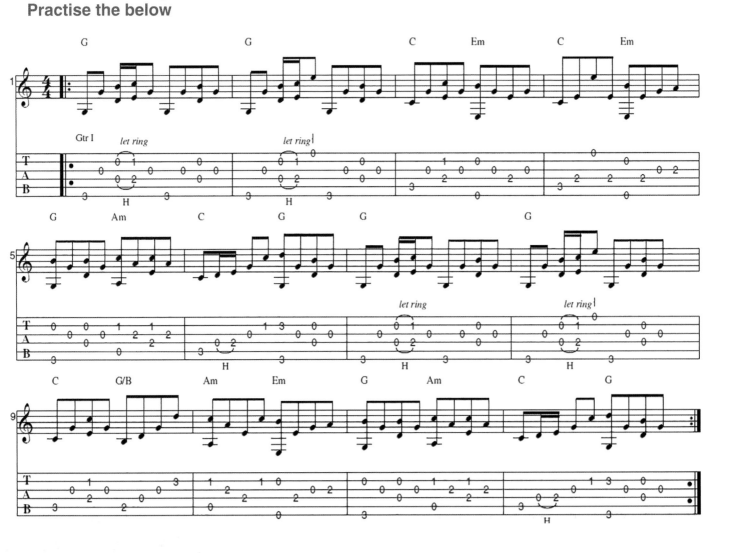

Country

Few genres sound as natural as country music, and it sure is great to roll back the years...

Country music has been around for almost a century now. During this time, the genre has undergone many changes, but one instrument has always been at the heart of it: the guitar. Whether it's acoustic like on Johnny Cash records, or the electric 'twang' that can be heard from Waylon Jennings, the guitar is surely the most important instrument in country music's sound. Indeed, it produces the high-treble twang that many associate with the genre - it's an instantly recognisable sound even to novices.

Musically, country borrows heavily from blues and folk music, so time signatures and chord structures are kept simple. A common strumming pattern in county music - one which you will have heard

TOP TIP

Mix in hammer-ons

Try bringing a finger down on a fret higher than the one being played to produce a second note from just one pick. This is a hammer-on (see page 54). Use the tab below to practise with open string to 2nd fret hammer-ons.

often on records - is to pick the bass string of the chord on the first beat before strumming the rest on the second. Try this with A minor, picking the open A and open E strings on beats 1 and 3 respectively.

Country essentials

These accessories walk a narrow line...

Resonator guitar

Get an old-school country sound with a resonator guitar, which produces an acoustic tone unlike anything else.

Thumbpicks

They take some getting used to, but masters of country music use thumbpicks to create a classic country sound.

83CB Capo

Many country music legends use capos. Shorten the fretboard without changing your sound with this one from Jim Dunlop.

Phosphor Bronze strings

If you're playing on an acoustic, make sure you've got a new set of strings to get the best sound.

Neil Young
Take inspiration from a country musician

Neil Young's early albums were dominated by his unique blend of country, folk and rock punctuated by his idiosyncratic guitar style heavily showcased in the extensive solos in Like a Hurricane and Down by the River performed on his iconic 1953 Gibson Les Paul dubbed 'Old Black'.

But it was Neil's acoustic work that brought him chart-topping fame with Harvest. He made extensive use of the Clawhammer banjo picking technique adapted for guitar, showcased on Old Man and Tell Me Why. His wide use of hammer-ons would bring character to simple progressions, alongside his distinctive harmonica playing that would give us the style many came to love. Keep this is mind when you try out the tabs below.

Give it a try
Practise the below

Blues

One of the oldest musical genres, blues is steeped in tradition, and presents a tough but rewarding challenge to play

As one of the most popular genres of all time, blues music is steeped in a rich history.

Blues is the music of the African-Americans from the Deep South, with its roots intertwined with African musical traditions, work songs and folk music, often incorporating chants and ballads. Since its origins in the late 19th Century, the world has seen many influential blues guitarists, from the likes of Robert Johnson and BB King to Jimi Hendrix and Eric Clapton.

Blues is often characterised by a slow tempo (usually around 60 to 90 beats per minute) and a standard I - IV - V chord progression (E - A - B if you're playing in E), usually with seventh chords thrown in. This progression is by no means mandatory for a blues piece, but if you familiarise yourself with the genre's songs and records, you'll notice that many blues numbers use it.

Guitar solos are also common in blues music, and the genre has scales that you can use over the aforementioned progression. These contain 'blue notes', a note played at a lower pitch than that of a major scale. For example, if you were playing blues in C, a blue note of F sharp or G flat would give you a distinctly bluesy sound.

> *"The world has seen many influential blues guitarists, from Robert Johnson to Eric Clapton"*

Blues essentials
Get that bluesy sound

BD-2 pedal
If you're looking for the much-sought-after creamy yet crunchy blues tone, check out this fantastic effects pedal from Boss.

Marshall Bluesbreaker II
If the BD-2 is a little out of your budget range, try out the Bluesbreaker II from Marshall.

Guitar slide
Achieve a different yet still bluesy sound by playing guitar with a slide. You are able to buy them in either brass or glass.

Peavey Classic 30
This may be a little bit on the expensive, side, but you will struggle to find a better blues amplifier for the same price.

Peter Green
Take inspiration from…

Peter Green made his name playing with John Mayall & the Bluesbreakers, before leaving to form Fleetwood Mac in 1967. While initially sticking to blues covers, he would soon write instantly recognisable classics like Black Magic Woman, Albatross, and the portentous The Green Manalishi. Peter Green was lauded for his legendary guitar sound, leading BB. King to say "He has the sweetest tone I ever heard", which is most prominent on The Supernatural.

Give it a try
Practise the below

TOP TIP

Placement & phrasing

Playing the blues isn't about trying to fill every gap with notes, instead you should try to place every note and bend with feeling and soul. Just as important is your 'phrasing' — the grouping of riffs and breaks to form musical phrases.

Jazz

Contrary to popular belief, jazz isn't confined to the saxophone — you can make sweet music on your guitar, too

© OhWeh

As it's one of the most complex musical genres in the world, playing jazz is a real test of a guitarist's ability.

Like the genre in general, jazz guitarists rarely stick to any musical templates or standards — any time signature or chord structure goes! Relatively simple chords like major sevenths (maj7) are very common, but commonly used chord types include augmented sevenths and minor ninths, which are rarely played in other types of popular music.

In terms of tone, guitars are often kept clean, with few effects added. Hammer-ons and pull-offs are exceptionally common, and there's a heavy emphasis on improvised solos (not just on lead guitar) to give jazz its whimsical sound. One of the masters of jazz guitar solos, Grant Green, whose style we have studied below, rarely recorded a song under five-minutes long, so his lengthy solos had to be varied to be kept interesting — yet he always remained in control of his instrument.

> *"Like the genre in general, jazz guitarists rarely stick to any musical templates or standards - any time signature or chord structure goes!"*

Jazz essentials
Look the part

Jazz strings
Try Jazz strings from D'Addario to get a great jazz sound. We recommend lights, but the mediums are a good option, too.

Jazz guitar
A distinctive jazz guitar will help you get a smooth, jazzy tone. The AS73 from Ibanez is great for beginners.

Lunchbox amp
The small-but-loud ZT Lunchbox really is a perfect amplifier for jazz. Its portability is another big bonus.

Hard case
Hollow and semi-hollow jazz guitar bodies aren't the strongest of instruments, so make sure you protect them with a hard case.

Grant Green
Take inspiration from a jazz musician

Grant Green's lengthy blues-tinged guitar solos are one of the most recognisable sounds in jazz. Although like many talented musicians he left us too soon (he was only 43 when he died of a heart attack), his music has lived on and influenced many modern jazz artists. There were jazz guitarists who had mastered more scales and could play quicker, but Green stuck to what he knew and, as such, became a master of memorable hooks and phrases. You're unlikely to find hundreds of notes in Green's solo; instead, the same phrase will often be repeated over again, often with subtle changes to keep the listeners on their toes.

TOP TIP

Improvise

Improvising is key to jazz, but the good news is that there aren't too many rules in jazz improvisation. Try to focus on the notes' phrasing, rather than the notes themselves. Sticking to the pentatonic scale will likely give you a more bluesy sound.

Give it a try
Practise the below

Classical

It takes serious skill to master the art of classical guitar-playing, so be prepared for a challenge

It may have never cracked the mainstream or topped the charts, but classical guitar music is incredibly popular with certain audiences, and is one of the most difficult genres for an artist to master. With its intricate finger-picking patterns and often complex arpeggios, classical guitar players require both hands to be at their most precise, and it's certainly a genre that requires a fair bit of patience and practise.

Classical duets/quartets are fairly common in this musical genre, but often guitarists are soloists, so they need to be picking bass notes as well as a higher-pitched melody. This results in interesting chord shapes occurring and finger patterns that are not seen in any other genre of music.

Classical guitars have nylon strings, are easier to play than steel-stringed guitars and are either acoustic or semi-acoustic. The traditional classical guitar has 12 frets clear of the body and is held on the left leg, so that the hand that plucks or strums the strings

© Fabricio Mattos

does so near the back of the soundhole. The modern steel string guitar, on the other hand, usually has 14 frets clear of the body and is commonly played off the hip. Low-end classical guitars are also incredibly cheap and a lot more gentle on the fingers, which is why many choose them as their first guitar. Many classical guitarists focus on arpeggios/broken chords rather than the regular chords heard in many other genres.

> **"Classical guitar is one of the most difficult genres to master"**

Classical essentials
Be prepared for the genre's intricacies

Nylon-stringed guitar
The classical sound can be achieved with nylon strings. The Fender ESC105 is great for beginners.

Spare strings
Always keep a spare set of strings on you. They're not always in high-street shops, so be prepared to search.

Arpeggios book
Classical guitarists need to know their arpeggios. A reference book such as this will help you create them.

Foot stool
A vital accessory for any classical guitarist, this makes it easier for the player to fret higher up the fretboard.

John Williams
Take inspiration from a classical musician

The fact that BRIT-Award-winning classical guitarist John Williams is considered a legend despite not being the most famous musician with the same name is testament to his talent with a classical guitar. Dealing mainly in arpeggiated chords and beautiful melodies on a nylon-stringed guitar, his tone is softer than other classical guitarists', so turn the treble down on a semi-acoustic. All four fingers of your fretting hand are vital to emulate Williams' style — some stretches he makes with his little finger are amazing!

© Getty

Try a foot stool

A key accessory in a classical guitarist's gig bag is a foot stool. One foot is perched on a stool to enable the guitarist to rest the instrument on a knee, which makes it easier to fret the irregular finger patterns found in classical guitar music.

Give it a try
Practise the below

Pop

If you fancy having a go at something a little bit more relaxed, why not give some pop chords a try?

The guitar has been a staple part of popular music for many years now, from the rock and roll of Elvis Presley and The Beatles' early catalogue to more modern acts like James Blunt, Maroon 5 and Pink. British pop rock band McFly, with their catchy and poppy melodies, became the youngest band ever to have an album debut at number one in 2004 - a title that they nabbed from The Beatles themselves.

Although most of today's pop bands and musicians are gradually incorporating more and more synthesised and electronic instruments into their acts, the successes of these acts — like Maroon 5 and McFly mentioned above — in this past decade proves that more traditional instruments still have their place in popular music and in the charts.

When it comes to playing pop music, there are a couple of chord progressions that you can try out to get started in the genre. E, G, D, A is one of the simplest progressions, yet this structure has

© Llapissera

been responsible for many of the most catchy pop songs in history. If you're proficient in barre chords, try Am, C, F, G as well. Keep your tone clean (adding in a little distortion in the chorus is also a common occurrence in pop music) and a key change of a semitone in the chorus is also used (E, G, D, A turns into F, G#, D# and A#) on the final chorus.

> ## "Traditional instruments still have their place in popular music and in the charts"

Pop essentials
The pieces of kit you need to play pop on your guitar

Wah-wah pedal
The wah-wah gives you a funky sound similar to Maroon 5. Jim Dunlop's selection of Crybabys are among the best.

Mic stand pick holder
The vocal harmonies mean you will likely end up singing — clip one of these to your mic stand!

4-Chord Songbook
See just how many of today's pop hits are based on just four chords with one of these handy, gig-bag-sized songbooks.

Digital delay pedal
You can create fantastic effects that could rival a keyboard with the help of the DD-3 digital delay pedal from Boss.

James Blunt
Take inspiration from…

As a captain in the British Army, Blunt nurtured his talent for performance and songwriting while on tour during the Kosovo War. Leaving the army in 2002 to pursue a career in music, Blunt drew scant recognition until the release of You're Beautiful, which launched him into the limelight, with his debut album Back To Bedlam going on to sell 11 million copies worldwide.

Blunt makes good use of simple, catchy melodies building to the big chorus, which has long been the cornerstone of pop music. This can be heard on Bonfire Heart, Wisemen and When I Find Love Again.

© Getty

Strum with a thin nylon pick

Vocals are the main focal point of a pop song, so it is important not to drown them out. But strumming softly can often remove energy from a song. A good solution to this is to use a thin nylon pick. Somewhere between 0.46mm and 0.71mm is perfect for a continuous strumming rhythm.

Give it a try
Practise the below

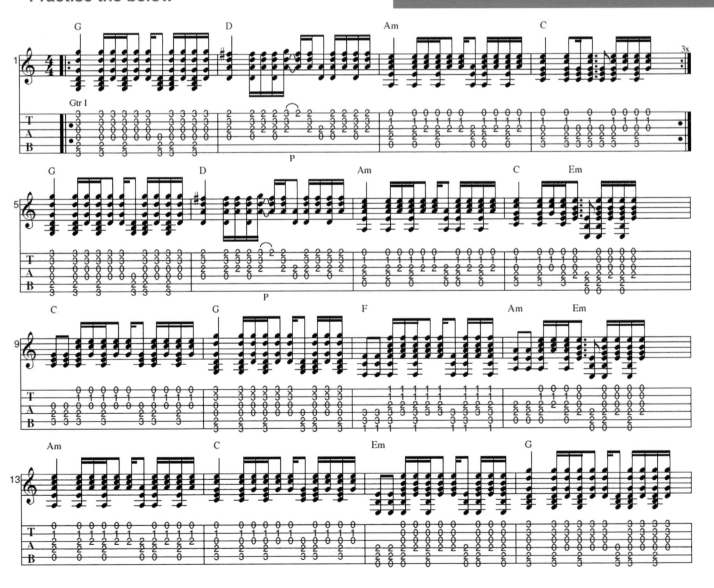

Helpdesk

Some final pointers to help you learn the guitar:
your common questions answered, a comprehensive
glossary and an essential chords list

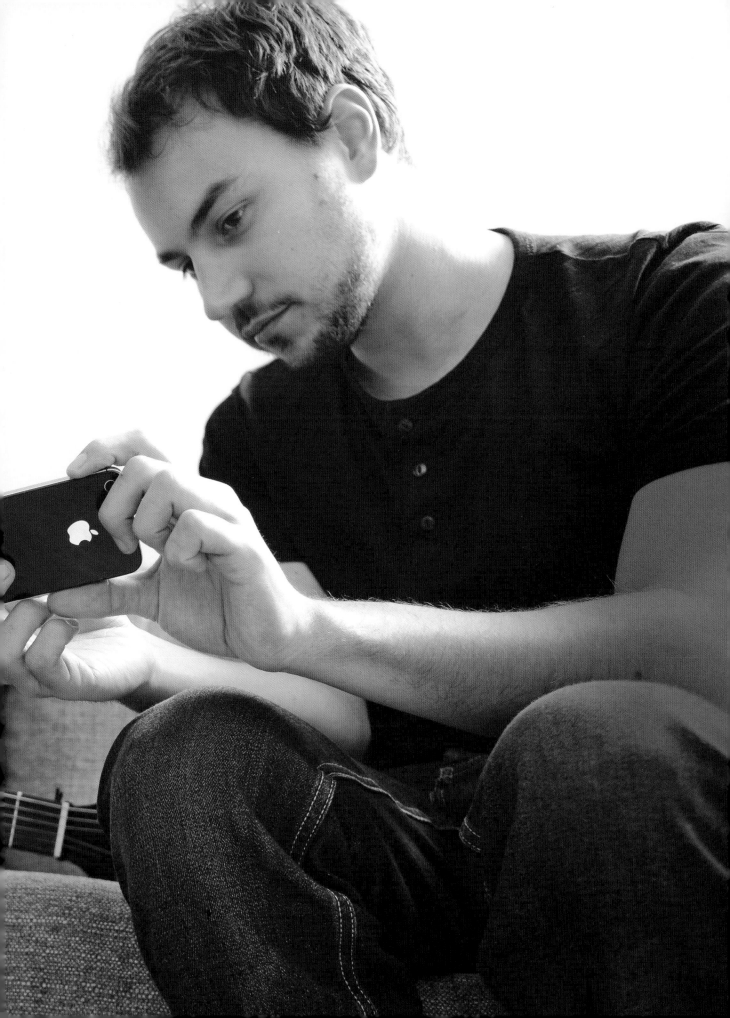

Your questions answered

Getting started

**So you've just bought a guitar and want to know what to do next?
Well here we guide you through the basics**

The learning timetable

I have no musical background and have recently considered picking up a guitar for the first time, so I was wondering how long it would take me to be able to play properly?

That all depends on how you define 'properly'. Some things can be learned quickly — such as the ability to strum along to simple songs — but the more complex stuff, such as crowd-pleasing solos, will take much longer. After picking up a guitar for the first time you will be aiming to play basic chords, not necessarily memorised but fretted and strummed, after about a week. The next two weeks will be spent mastering and memorising the basic chords to the point where you can play one or two songs without having to look at the fretboard while you strum and switch between chords. After two months you should have learned and mastered the ability to play barre and power chords, then in the next month mastered finger picking — the ability to play individual strings.

Then, depending on how quickly you learn and how much you practise, you'll move onto riffs within about four months and put everything you've learned thus far together to be able to improvise riffs and solos within a year.

No pain, no gain

People often say that the biggest problem when learning the guitar is the pain in your fingers. Is this true? Will my fingers hurt when I first start learning to play guitar?

If you're completely new to guitar and have never fretted a string before there will undoubtedly be some level of discomfort involved. During the first week or so, the tips of your four fretting fingers will feel tender and sore as you press down on the strings, and your fingers may ache at being contorted into positions they aren't accustomed to, but the discomfort will subside fairly quickly. By playing for at least 30 minutes every day, you will soon develop calluses on the tips of your fingers. Though this may sound worrying, it essentially just means that the skin is hardening up over time, and once this guitar-playing evolution occurs, you'll find that you will be able to fret the strings with no discomfort at all for the rest of your playing days.

You could be rocking solo licks in under a year

Your fingers will adapt to pressure

Guitar choice
Should I learn to play on acoustic or electric?

This is very much down to personal preference. Some learners find it easier to finger pick on an acoustic guitar and, indeed, the thicker strings and wider neck mean that you get accustomed to the discomfort of fretting strings and contorting your fingers into chord formations much quicker. If you learn on an acoustic and then moving onto an electric, you will find it easier to implement everything you've learned on the new instrument as the neck is much thinner so forming the chords is easier. Ultimately, though, the best guitar to learn on is the one you wish to continue using. So if you want to pick up an electric and go straight onto power chords, that's fine — everything you learn will benefit you in the long term.

Common problems
What are the common problems that new learners encounter?

The most obvious one is a feeling of frustration and a desire to pack it in! Whether this stems from the discomfort newcomers feel in their hands when adjusting to the demands of fretting strings and forming chords, or the feeling that you aren't progressing as quickly as you'd like, the important thing is to stick with it. It is important to master the basics before moving on to trickier things such as solos, otherwise you risk developing bad technique.

Choosing your weapon
What type of guitar is best for learners? And what should I be looking out for when considering which guitar to buy?

Again, there is no simple answer, but you should familiarise yourself with the different types of guitar to determine what is best for you before making any purchases. Classical guitars use nylon strings and have large fretboards. This means that the strings are smoother on your fingers and they are also further apart. But it's not one of the most popular genres and it is probably sensible to only pick up a classical guitar if you are looking to focus on that genre. Acoustic guitars are similar to classical guitars but have steel strings that produce a louder sound. The drawback is that acoustic guitars are harder on the fingers but their necks are thinner, making them better suited to smaller hands. Acoustic-electric guitars can, as the name suggests, be played with or without an amp and come with a built-in pickup that sometimes includes tuner controls, making them easier to get perfectly in tune. Electric guitars have narrow necks and the strings are easier to press down, making them easier for beginners to get used to. However, they have little natural sound of their own and so will always require an amp.

> *"It is important to master the basics before moving onto tricker things such as solos"*

Tuning up
I was recently given a second-hand guitar as a gift and I would like to start teaching myself to play. How do I know if my guitar needs tuning and how do I go about tuning it?

The more accomplished you get at playing the guitar, the more trained your ears will become in telling if it is in tune or not. As such, you will get to the stage where you'll be able to tune it by ear. The notes played on the open strings of your guitar should rise up through a scale, so you'll instantly be able to tell if one or more strings are out of tune.

There is a method of tuning your guitar manually, but you will need a reference to tune your sixth string (the low E), which can be with a tuning fork or piano. When your sixth string is in tune, play the sixth string on the fifth fret (A) and then tune your open fifth string (A) to sound the same. Next, play the fifth string on the fifth fret (D), and then tune your open fourth string (D) to sound the same. Play the fourth string on the fifth fret (G) and then tune your open third string (G) to sound the same. Play the third string on the fourth fret (B) and tune your open second string (B) to sound the same. Finally, play the second string on the fifth fret (E) and then tune your open first string (E) to sound the same. Bear in mind that there are plenty of good free tuning apps available for your smartphone and tuners you can buy too.

Improve your speed with the help of a metronome

What is a metronome?

I have read about using a metronome while practising. What is a metronome and how can it help my playing?

A metronome is a device that counts time by producing regular sounds. This is a useful tool when you need to practise at a certain tempo or if you're trying to increase your speed on the guitar. The tempo of a metronome is measured in beats per minute (BPM) and metronomes come in three forms — mechanical, electrical and software. A traditional metronome is a triangular device that holds a metal ticker with a slider through which you can adjust the speed.

Most modern metronomes are electronic, but follow the same basic principle and use electronics and quartz crystal to maintain the beat. Metronomes are useful for practising scales and increasing your speed. You may only be able to play a scale at 90bpm at first, but by practising with a metronome and increasing the tempo at which you practise every day with, say 5bpm, you will train your fingers and brain to play quicker. It is also possible to get metronome apps for your smartphone that work just as well as the more traditional models.

"A metronome counts time by producing regular sounds"

Positioning your guitar strap
I am just starting out with an electric guitar and want to know how high I should set my strap?

Start off by adjusting the strap so that the back plate of the guitar is level with your pelvis. Play a few chords to see if it feels comfortable.

You don't want the guitar set too high or you'll be tied up with tension trying to play appropriately and it will hurt your hands.

The opposite is also true — strap your guitar too low and you'll have a hard time getting your hands in the right positions to fret and pick.

Your guitar
You'll want to know all about your instrument as you learn to play it

Changing the strings

How often should I change the strings of my guitar? I have heard conflicting answers but am unsure as the strings on my guitar have been on there for a couple of years at least, so how do I know if they need changing?

Ultimately, your ears will tell you when they need replacing. Over time, dirt and oil from your hands will build up on your strings, causing them to become tarnished and start to sound dull and lifeless. Washing your hands prior to playing will help prolong the life of your strings, but other factors, such as the natural stretching of the string over time, will require you to change your strings regularly. You will know if your strings need changing if you have a harder time than usual getting your guitar in tune (and, in turn, keeping it in tune), if the tone of your guitar starts to sound flat or if the strings begin to discolour or rust. So, if you play often, you may need to change the strings every several months. There are also a few common factors to take into account to determine how regularly your strings need to be changed. For example, guitarists who sweat more will need to change strings more often, guitarists who smoke or play in smoky venues will need to change their strings more often, and guitarists who play aggressively and dish out more punishment on their strings will need to change them more regularly than gentler players. When buying new strings, be aware that they come in varying gauges (which is the thickness) and you will find that the lighter-gauged strings are much easier to fret.

Guitar brand

What brand of guitar do you recommend for beginners and how do I know what to look for when buying?

When starting out, it is probably best to avoid the more expensive brands such as Gibson or Fender (unless laying out big bucks is a motivator for ensuring that you stick with it) and go for a decent entry-level guitar. This way, if you really do decide that playing guitar isn't for you, you won't be left licking your financial wounds for months to come. Brands to look out for when buying your first guitar include Encore, Epiphone, First Act, Squier and Yamaha, and when browsing, you should always make a point of playing each guitar you look at (it also helps to drag a guitar-playing friend along).

Ensure that the guitars you are browsing are tuned to concert pitch or standard tuning to allow you to compare models better, and play each one sitting and standing to ensure that they feel comfortable. A good trick of the trade is to place your index finger directly behind the first fret (the raised metal line) on the biggest string and then pluck the string. Listen out for odd noises and then repeat the process on each fret and each string. If you hear of any buzzes or other non-musical noises, ask the assistant to retune the guitar and if the problem persists, that guitar is definitely no-go.

Why change the strings?

I have heard that it is a good idea to replace the strings on a newly-purchased guitar as soon as you buy it. But if the whole thing is new then why should I do this?

For a couple of reasons. Most new guitars leave the factory strung with generic-type strings, which are fine for tinkering with in the shop, but if you want a clearer, richer sound then you'll be amazed at how different a decent set of brand-name strings will sound. After all, the existing strings could have been on there for years and be worn out and corroded — and just imagine how many other sets of hands have had a good twang on them before you! Guitar strings lose quality gradually over time the more they are played and tuned down and up again, so if you want your guitar to sound as good as it possibly can, then a new set of strings will make all the difference for your instrument.

Feeling the buzz

I have noticed that my electric guitar is making a strange buzzing sound when I pluck the strings. I have only started to notice this noise recently, so I was wondering if there was any logical reason behind it?

This occurs when your strings vibrate against the fretboard when plucked. It may be that you simply aren't holding the strings down firmly enough, or it may be something more sinister.

Ensure that your strings are tuned properly. An electronic tuner will ensure that your strings aren't too loose and rule this out. Ideally, you want your strings to be as close to the fretboard as possible for a lower action (this is the distance between the strings and the fretboard). But if the action on your guitar is so low that it causes the strings to vibrate against the frets, it would be a good idea to take your guitar to a music store and get a qualified technician to take a look at it. You should also check if the neck of your guitar is bent. If it is, adjust the truss rod on the neck with an Allen key.

Techniques

Once you've mastered the basics and grown accustomed to your instrument, it's time to develop your playing further

Improving your strumming

My sense of rhythm is appalling and, as such, my basic strumming technique is all over the shop. Do you have any good tips or tricks for bringing new vibrancy to my strumming?

One of the main ways to bring new life and energy to otherwise routine songs is using an interesting strumming pattern. To practise your strumming, form a G chord on your fretting hand and then strum down and up on the strings while counting out loud, "one and two and three and four" — the numbers being a downward stroke and the "and" being upward. This will help you keep to a steady time. Also it is wise not to strum too hard as this will cause the strings to rattle. Think of your elbow as being the top of a pendulum — your arm should swing up and down from it in a steady motion, never pausing at any time.

I've heard of artificial harmonics — what are they?

I have heard of a technique called artificial harmonics. Is there such a thing as natural harmonics, and how do I produce the artificial kind on my guitar?

Natural harmonics are created when your finger is directly above the desired fret and you are barely touching the string. Immediately after picking the string, come away from it and it should ring quite a bit higher than normal. Artificial harmonics are when you strike the string with the picking hand's thumb as you cross the string with your hand. This is usually done in a downward motion and depends on where you are picking. To do this, grip the tip of your pick so that when you strike the string it catches your thumb and you will hear a harmonic generated over the initial note. This technique sounds best on an electric guitar used with an amplifier but it can work on an acoustic-electric and acoustic guitar too.

Bring out harmonics for a twist on the usual notation

Fingernail maintenance
What's the best way to groom my fingernails for guitar playing?

Classic guitar players like to keep the nails on their fretting hand short and those on their strumming hand long. The reason for this is because the nail is 50 per cent responsible for the tone and volume of their instrument and also aids speed and accuracy while playing.

So while having long nails is by no means essential, it can certainly help — and they don't have to be too long. The ideal length can be determined by holding your hand flat in front of your face with the palm facing inwards. If you can just see the nails protruding over the top of your fingertips your nails are the perfect length for easy finger picking.

Exercising both hands
Why is it important to develop the technique of both hands for playing?

If you are concentrating purely on your fretwork, a lot of the subtleties of playing the guitar are lost. Both hands are equally important and if you want to become a more accomplished player you shouldn't ignore practising and developing techniques for your strumming hand. As such, never rely on a pick alone to strum the strings, make sure you use your fingers to get a feel for them and work on a few arpeggios to give your playing hand a thorough work out at the start of each session.

Thumbs up?
I have heard plenty of conflicting views on the correct position of the thumb on your fretting hand while playing. So where exactly should it be?

Some think the thumb should be pressed against the back of the neck and others say it's fine to rest the flat of the thumb on top. Either is fine really — you should position your thumb in a place that

It is important to keep both hands limber

aids your playing. The latter method does mean that the thumb can be used as a fretting tool if needs be.

What are ghost notes?
I have heard the term ghost notes. What are these exactly and how would I go about playing them on my electric guitar?

Think of ghost notes as notes that are felt but not heard. Ultimately, ghost notes are what we call artificial harmonics. These are harmonics that are generated by picking a string with both your pick and your thumb. This causes the note and a harmonic (an octave above the note) to sound. This can be done on any guitar, electric or acoustic, although most people are familiar with this technique through playing an electric guitar. Depending on your tone settings, amp and effects, ghost notes can cause quite an intense, eerie sound and are good for fleshing out your compositions and adding more depth.

In terms of your guitar settings, the best way to set things up is to plug your guitar into the amp and sit as far away from it as your cable will allow. Now, starting with one dial on your guitar, experiment by tweaking it a little and then playing a chord. Take note of the sound and then move the dial some more to get your preferred result. Don't forget to experiment with the dials on your amp too. Small, subtle adjustments can make a big difference to the sound that comes out and, if you are a performing guitar player, you'll want to ensure that your guitar is set to the levels that make it sound best prior to taking to the stage and rocking out.

Warming up both hands puts you in the best position to play

Stopping unwanted noise

I have started playing solos on my electric guitar and am having a hard time keeping all the lower strings from ringing out while soloing on the higher ones. How can I mute unwanted noise?

There are a couple of methods for muting the unwanted noise of strings ringing out, the most popular one with beginners being to try muting the lower strings with the palm of your picking hand.

However, we have discovered down the years that the most reliable technique for muting unwanted noise if you accidentally hit the lower strings while soloing is to use the thumb of your picking hand. Basically, the thumb rests on all of the lower strings — lower down than where the pick is. For example, if the pick is currently playing a note on the B string, then the thumb would be muting (touching) the G, D, A and low E strings. The high E string would be muted by one of the fingers on the fretting hand, usually the first finger. Practising this thumb-muting technique can be frustrating at times and may feel slightly unnatural at first but the effort will be worth it and it will eventually come naturally to you.

The biggest problem to overcome is the new positioning of your picking hand. If you are used to muting with the palm then it will undoubtedly feel awkward to reposition your picking hand so that it is more parallel with the strings. The best solution is to stop trying to rest the palm on or near the bridge of the guitar. Yes it will feel strange and alien at first but the more you practise using this technique, the easier it will become.

Skilful soloing

I am struggling to improve my soloing skills and wondered if you had any tips to help?

> *"A reliable technique for muting unwanted noise is to use the thumb of your picking hand"*

We know speed isn't everything, but set a metronome at a tempo that you feel comfortable with and practise scale runs, triplets or quadruplets. Increase the tempo gradually in order to push your boundaries.

Ensure you nail the accuracy. The only way to do this is to go through the passage slowly playing every note until you have them all correct and ingrained into your visual and muscle memory. In short, don't rush.

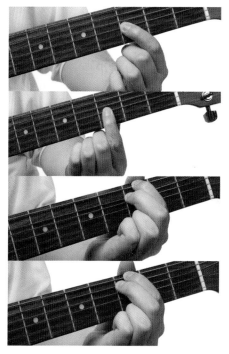

A useful exercise is to pick four notes and play them in a different sequence repeatedly to help improve your speed and stretch your fingers. Often you can find great melodic lines by just fooling around in this way.

Reading music

There is no law that says you have to be able to read music to play guitar, but it can definitely prove beneficial to your playing

Learning to read

I am a complete musical novice who has just picked up a guitar and I was wondering if I should start learning how to read music to help improve my playing?

While learning to read music will undoubtedly stand you in better stead moving forward and developing, it is by no means essential — some of the greatest guitarists of all time can't read a note. That said, it's really not hard, and by doing so you will be able to learn new songs and develop much quicker. For example, by reading music you aren't just limiting yourself to guitar music, you can get some really good ideas and arrangements from being able to read piano music. One of the best things about music is the way in which you can borrow certain elements from different disciplines and adapt them for your own purposes. This could be borrowing an arrangement from piano sheet music or adapting horn parts or fiddle tunes to use and reinterpret in your own musical arrangements. The flexibility that being able to read music affords you shouldn't be underestimated when you are considering the benefits of putting in the time and effort. Ultimately, though, whether you decide to learn to read music or not, you should continue to enjoy playing guitar on whatever terms.

Terrifying terminology

I know nothing about guitar terminology — can you tell me what chords, scales, barre chords and power chords are?

A guitar chord is a collection of tones or notes played together at once. By fretting (pressing down on) the strings in certain places, guitar chords are formed and you play them by strumming all the strings at once. For example, if you press down on a string and pluck it, the sound that comes out is a note. If you are pressing several strings down at once and strumming them then the sound that is played is called a chord.

A scale is a collection of notes in ascending or descending order. If you want to progress on to playing solos and riffs, scales are the perfect place to start because they strengthen your fingers with practise, developing your picking technique and helping your co-ordination. Barre chords require you to press down on multiple strings with your index finger on a single fret. Barre chords are more difficult for beginners to play since they require more strength and effort from your fretting hand. A power chord, in most cases, is nothing more than a barre chord where you only play two or three strings instead of strumming all of them together. Read more about barre chords on page 42.

Persevere for perfect barre chords

Struggling with barres

I have been playing guitar for a while and am now starting to learn barre chords. However, I am struggling to contort my hand into positions that don't feel natural, so is there an easy way to learn barre chords?

In a word, no. Barre chords are notoriously hard, but there are a couple of handy pointers you can take note of. If you look at your index finger, it has a slight bend in it, which leaves the middle of the barre hard to press down. Rotate your finger slightly so that the knuckle is facing the top of the guitar and this will flatten the finger, making it easier for you to barre the strings.

You will need to develop muscles that you have probably never used before, so keep at it!

> "Drop D tuning is perhaps most widely used by guitarists in the metal genre"

Lowering the tone

I have heard of something called drop D tuning from my other guitar-playing friends. What is drop D tuning and how does it differ from standard guitar tuning?

Drop D tuning is an alternative guitar tuning where the sixth or lowest string is tuned down, or dropped, one tone (which equates to two frets) to D rather than E. When using drop D tuning, the three bass strings form a D5 power chord when played openly. Fretting the three bass strings on the same fret naturally provides a simple way to play power chords, which helps some guitarists play particular styles of music.

For example, drop D tuning is perhaps most widely used by guitarists in the metal genre, as guitarists who play this style often need to make extremely fast transitions between different power chords. Tuning your guitar this way will also benefit you if you favour playing blues or country-style music. Ultimately, drop D tuning isn't something you need to consider until you master all of the basics of guitar playing and then adopt your own favoured style — it's just a useful shortcut to help you make quick and easy transitions between chords when you become a more accomplished player. Read about playing in the style of metal and drop D tuning on page 116.

Beginning with barre chords

Which barre chord shape should I begin learning and how should I practise switching from chord to chord?

The first shape you should learn to play is E minor because it is one of the easiest. It involves pressing down the fifth and fourth strings (A and D) two frets ahead of your barring finger with your ring and little finger respectively.

From E minor, you can progress fairly easily to E major, which simply involves pressing your middle finger down on the third string (G) on the first fret after your barre and keeping your third and fourth fingers on the A and D strings.

A minor has the same fingering as E major as it uses the same shape; you're just moving your hand over one string — so you're holding down the D and G strings on the second fret after your barre and the B string on the first fret.

"Don't run before you can walk. Familiarise yourself with a few chord structures at a time"

Practising

Practice is vital if you want to progress as a guitarist, so here we look at ways that you could improve your playing over time

Practice makes perfect

I don't seem to be getting any better; how much time should I spend practising?

The obvious answer is however much time you can spare, but we'd recommend at least half an hour a day to condition your fingers and make sure you don't forget anything. If you know some chords then you already know enough to strum quite a few simple songs and play some simple riffs. You also know enough to start writing and playing some of your own songs, so there are plenty of avenues open to you.

The important thing to remember is not to run before you can walk. Familiarise yourself with a few chord structures at a time and then work on making the transition between them sound as seamless as possible — getting good, clean contact on the strings so that they don't buzz and swift movement without looking at what your fretting hand is doing. As soon as you have mastered a decent array of chords you'll be able to start playing songs, which is immensely satisfying because you have a clear gauge on how far you will have progressed as a player. Once you can play songs you can also start improvising and adding little licks here and there to flesh them out beyond the chords.

Basic songs

I would like to learn some songs. Could you recommend some easy ones?

Okay, one of the easiest songs to learn is House Of The Rising Sun by The Animals. This song comprises only five chords — and they're all easy to master. These consist of A minor, C major, D major, F major and E Major, which are all played on the first three frets with relatively simple transitions between them.

Simpler still is Horse With No Name, written by Dewey Bunnell of the group America. This song consists of just two chords — E minor (hold the A and D strings on the second fret) and Dadd6add9 (this basically involves splitting the same two fingers so that they hold the thick E and G string). Play this with a simple strumming pattern of one-and-two-and-three-and-four, with the "and" being the upward strum, in E minor then change to the same pattern in Dadd6add9. Other simple yet great-sounding songs to learn are Man On The Moon by REM, Scarborough Fair by Simon and Garfunkel and Nirvana's epic take on the Leadbelly song Where Did You Sleep Last Night?, as performed during their famous appearance on the MTV Unplugged television series.

What are arpeggios?

I have often heard of the term arpeggios being used in relation to guitar playing as a good method of warming up, but I don't know what they are or how they should sound. Please can you enlighten me?

Guitar arpeggios are indeed a useful and worthwhile limbering up exercise, but they can help you in the long term, too, by giving your solos some melodic and vivid parts.

Arpeggios are built up as regular guitar chords, but instead of letting all of the strings sound simultaneously, as you would normally do with chords, arpeggios are played by letting each note sound one at a time. For example, if you fret a chord — any chord — then a good, simple arpeggio can be played by picking each string in succession. To warm up your picking hand, fret a basic A major or A minor chord and use each finger of your picking hand to pluck a string. So, your thumb would pluck the A string, then your index finger would pick the D string, your middle finger would pick the G, and so on.

Repeat this sequence a couple of times and then change the chord with your fretting hand while continuing to play the sequence for a nice, smooth transition. Not only is this a great way to loosen up your fingers prior to a session, but it is also a useful exercise to help you get accustomed to picking individual strings. As you get more proficient at finger picking arpeggios, the less you will have to look down at your guitar as you play to ensure you're hitting the right string every time.

Professional help

In your opinion, what is the best method for learning guitar? Do I need a tutor or can I get by using books or DVDs?

You can get by quite happily using books or DVDs; in fact, we would heartily recommend doing so to begin with so that you can get accustomed to your instrument and ascertain if you like playing and wish to continue.

However, we have found that books and DVDs, while beneficial for helping you learn chords and strumming patterns, are no long-term substitute for a professional tutor. A good teacher can further your development quickly over a short space of time and prevent you from developing bad technique, which could hamper your playing further down the line. So if you can afford it, book lessons with a tutor, otherwise just continue enjoying your instrument, as you no doubt have been.

Recording

Professional studio recording will be out of reach for most beginners, but you can get great results by recording at home

Digital acoustic recording

I love playing my classical guitar, and I want to record some tracks with it. However, I want to edit them using a computer and obviously I can't plug the guitar into my machine directly because there are no pickups. How can I record acoustically on the computer?

It really depends on your available budget. The cheapest option would be to buy a USB desktop microphone and plug it into your computer. Make sure you stick the microphone near the soundhole of the guitar (but not so close that your fingers get in the way and pollute your recording) and record what the microphone hears into your favourite audio editor, like Apple's GarageBand or Audacity. A decent desktop microphone can be picked up for around £25/$39, or your computer may have one built in (but keep in mind you won't have much flexibility of movement in this case).

Another option open to you is to use a USB audio interface with a built-in mic to pick up your acoustic playing. If you use a Mac, the Apogee ONE can be bought for around £120/$180 second hand and comes highly recommended for beginners. The method of recording your acoustic guitar is the same, but you will notice a great difference in the quality of your recordings.

Mix it up

What is mixing, and is it important?

After you've finished recording all your guitar and backing tracks, you will need to mix them together to make it sound good, usually into a two-channel stereo. The bad news is that entire books have been written on this topic, so it's not an easy matter to get to grips with. To start with, you should edit the volume of each individual track until you're happy with the sound they all make. Once you've got that, you can start to pan your tracks to the left or right speaker if you feel it adds to the mix.

Tablet recording

Is recording using an iPad really a viable option for a decent result?

It certainly is, but you will need your fair share of apps and accessories for it to work, like the iRig that we covered earlier in this book. Many popular artists are using iOS's diverse range of music apps to create great sounds for their albums, but few are recording their entire record on the tablet.

The iPad does have a few things going in its favour, though. One is its portability, which means it can be taken anywhere with your music still on it. If you want to lay down a track in your lunch break then there's no better way of doing so, and iCloud support means you can carry on where you left off when you get home.

Backing tracks

My playing is improving and I feel I'm ready to join a rock band and record for a bigger sound. However, I'm struggling to join one, and I'm living in a small apartment, so I have no room for other instruments. Can I make a backing track for my guitar using a computer?

Most definitely! In fact, these days, it's far easier and cheaper to record synthesised instruments on a computer. All you need are some instrument plug-ins, many of which can be freely downloaded from the internet. If you're on Windows, you will probably want a VST; if you're on Mac, you'll want a VST or AU (audio unit). How you install these plug-ins depends on your audio editor, so search the program's help files for assistance.

When your plug-in is installed you can use a MIDI keyboard to play what you're looking for. If you don't have a MIDI keyboard, don't worry, as many editors enable you to control the VST with your computer keyboard. It must be said, however, that digital instruments are in no way a substitute for the real deal, but they do help those of us who have limited resources.

Sounding different

I just nailed the perfect take on my guitar, but it sounds dreadful when I play it back — what am I doing wrong?

The solution is usually a lot simpler than you may think. If you're recording through a microphone, make sure it's not too close to your guitar's soundhole or amp, or you may get an unwanted distortion effect. Also, be sure to check the volume of the

track on the computer — if it's +10dB it probably won't sound right.

In many recording programs, you can opt to monitor your guitar through headphones as you go. This way you can hear what your recording will sound like. Also, this will mean you can listen to a backing track without the mic picking it up. If you don't wear headphones, yet still monitor your guitar, you run the risk of creating cacophonous feedback, which will be captured by the microphone.

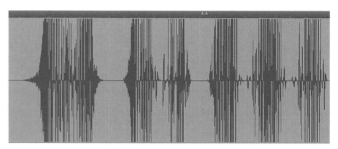

If your guitar recording looks like this, you may want to adjust the position of your microphone

"Guitar arpeggios are indeed a useful and worthwhile limbering up exercise, but they can help you in the long term, too"

Virtual effects wizard

I don't want to spend lots of money on pedals, but I still want to record my guitar with some funky effects. Is this possible?

We've already mentioned how VST instruments can enhance your sound, but now here's where VST effects come in handy. Whether you just want to add a subtle reverb effect or a crazy phaser, these plug-ins have got you covered. Like the instrumental, VST installing methods will vary depending on your audio editor, but it will likely be a similar process. Many VSTs will have multiple settings, but it is down to you to select the best ones, as there are several variables that affect the sound. Make sure you save once you've found the perfect settings.

However, just because you can use these effects on your computer doesn't mean that you should. For instance, if you ever plan on playing live, it is a far better idea to invest in pedals as it's not exactly easy to change effects halfway through a song if you've got to run to your computer and click a few buttons! Also, you would be missing out on effects like wah-wah and volume. There's no way to record a guitar part and control wah-wah at the same time — you only have one pair of hands!

Recording from distance

I love recording my electric guitar but I hate having to go back and forth between instrument and computer. Is there any way to solve this problem of mine?

If you record your guitar on a Mac, you're in luck. The Apogee GiO is a guitar interface that enables you to record your guitar in GarageBand or Logic via its stomp pads. Stomp on the Record button to start, the Fast Forward button to move through your recording and so on. This not only means that you don't have to keep moving from guitar to computer every time you want to hear a take, but also that you can keep your hands on your guitar and let your feet worry about the recording.

It also controls effects, so if you want to make use of your audio editor's built-in effects (or indeed the VST plug-ins we discussed in the previous question), just stomp away until you get the preset sound that you require. All you need to do is plug your guitar into it, just as you would a normal amp, then hook the interface up to your computer via a USB cable.

Sharing
As you create music, you may wish to share it with others — but how do you go about doing so?

Feedback needed

I've recorded a few basic riffs and played them to my friends. They're really into them, but I want to get more feedback on them before I develop the pieces into a full song. What's the best way that I can do this?

The internet makes it relatively easy to obtain feedback on your work. You could upload the riff to a forum that specialises in the genre of music you play, but these are often frequented by advanced amateurs and professionals, so their advice may not be too helpful if you're a beginner. A better bet would be to find beginner-focused websites and forums, as these will contain many like-minded individuals willing to help out and provide feedback. They'll also be able to offer feedback on your recording methods as well as your playing, so you can improve in several key areas. If you receive constructive negative feedback, make sure you use it to improve your recordings.

If you own an iPhone, iPad or iPod touch, a good way of getting feedback is to use an app such as Riff Raters. Riff Raters enables you to upload 20-second riffs to the app, which can then be rated out of five by members of the Riff Raters community. If your riff is rated highly enough, it will reach the feature top 25, where it will gain you even more exposure and feedback.

Upload a song

Are there any good websites to upload a song to? I don't want to spend anything in the process.

You're in luck, as there are several! The one that we would recommend is SoundCloud, which is a fantastic website to share your music on. Although it has many premium pricing options, the free service gives you two hours of music to upload, so unless you're a songwriting maniac just churning them out, you probably won't run out of minutes any time soon!

You can either share your track to every social networking service under the sun, or you can opt to share it to a SoundCloud group. If you share it to a group, make sure you pick one with interests similar to your genre, as you'll get far more listens that way. Listeners can also favourite and comment on your uploaded track.

A slightly more surprising option to get your songs on the web for free is YouTube. You can just upload audio to the site. Once your track is uploaded, add it as a video response to a popular track similar to yours. This ensures you get listens and likes. If you have the hardware and the confidence, why not record yourself on video?

Up for sale

How can I get my work up for sale on the big digital distribution services like iTunes? I'm working on writing an album and I want to know that when I'm done I can make some money from it.

You're best off looking at services like CD Baby and TuneCore, which will upload your music to all the major players in digital distribution, like iTunes, Amazon MP3 and Spotify, as well as selling it on their own site. Some services will charge a one-off fee and take a cut off each sale, while others will charge a yearly fee and let you keep all the profits.

However, once your music is on these services, the real work begins. Because of their insane popularity, it's highly unlikely that people will just stumble upon your music. You'll need to consider using social networking services like Twitter and Facebook to get the news out there.

Getting heard

I know internet radio is incredibly popular, so how can I get my music on a station? I know I won't be able to get on national radio, but there are so many stations out there and I'd love to be played on one.

Instead of sending your demo into DJs like in the old days, there are a few websites that enable you to you upload your music for the chance to be on their radio station. One such site is www. amazingtunes.com. By uploading your music, you stand the chance of being played on their very own Amazing Radio, which is on digital radio. They also have their own YouTube channel. It doesn't matter what genre you play either, as they have DJs who specialise in indie, ambient, folk and loads more in between. All their music is sourced from new or emerging artists and you can count yourself among them.

If you get selected to be played, you'll receive an email from the DJ telling you what show you'll be on — so be sure to tell everyone you know and everyone they know to listen in! Besides those people that you do tell, you'll never know who else might be listening.

A slightly less direct way of getting on the radio is through www. slicethepie.com. At Slice The Pie people can listen to and rate your music, and if they really like it they can choose to invest. If you get enough fans investing in your music, you will be in with a chance of being played, as well as having enough financial backing to take that giant leap and record your first album.

You can use various services to get your music on iTunes

Facebook fans
How can I get my band and music on Facebook? I want fans not friends!

Rather than sign up as a person by using the text fields, click Create a Page for a Celebrity, Band or Business below them.

Click Artist, Band or Public Figure, select Musician/Band, name yourself, then agree to the terms and conditions and click Get Started.

Now link it to your personal Facebook account if you so wish, and you'll have the chance to start adding fans and promoting your music!

Major chords

Get a happy sound with these shapes

Basic major chords are incredibly popular in Western guitar music, probably because many of them are easy to play and they give your songs a happy feel. These chords contain the first, third and fifth notes in the corresponding major scale. It's worth noting that the 'major' isn't often referred to when you see these chords written down.

Key

1 Index **2** Middle **3** Ring **4** Little **X:** Don't strum this string

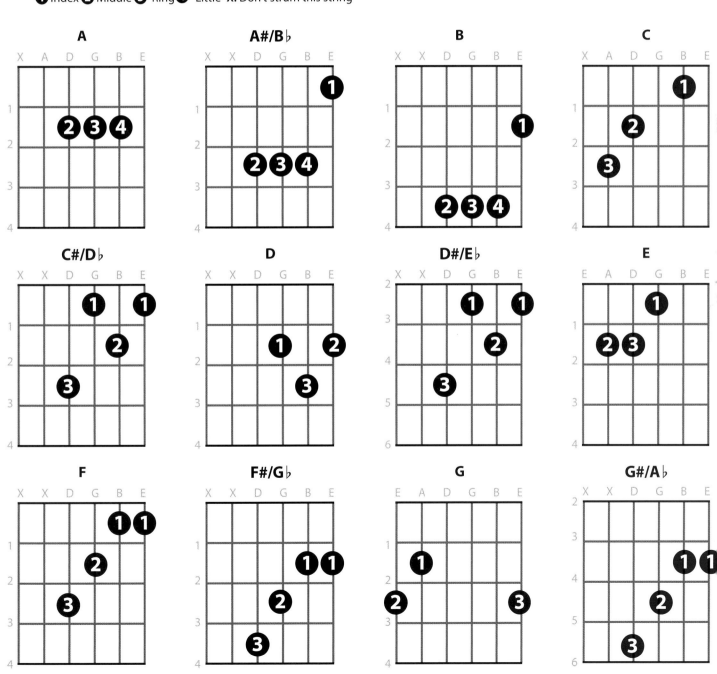

Minor chords

The best way to get a sad sound

A basic minor chord will give you a much sadder sound than a major chord. This is because the third note in the major scale is 'flattened' in pitch by one semitone. For example, 'E' is the third note in the C major scale (CDEFGAB), and this is flattened by a semitone to E♭ to give a C minor chord its distinct melancholy sound.

Key

1 Index **2** Middle **3** Ring **4** Little **X:** Don't strum this string

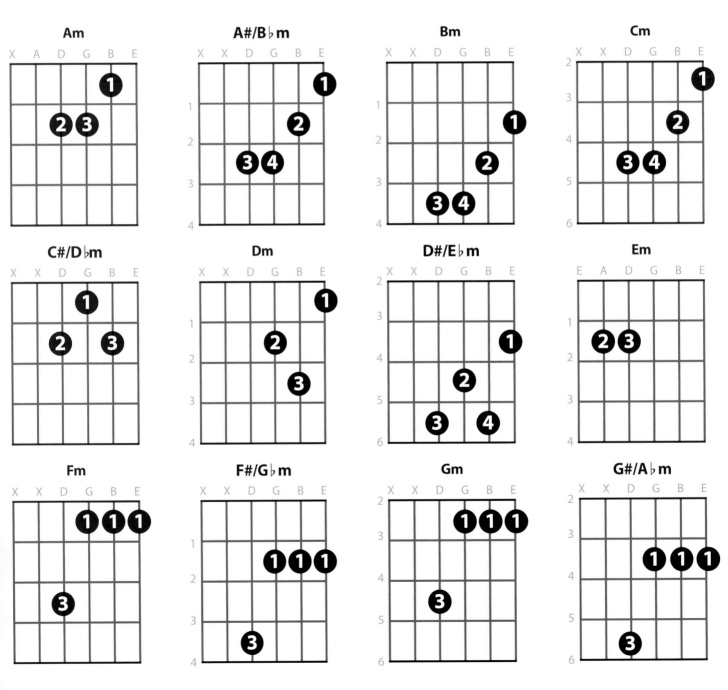

Dominant seventh chords

Improve your progressions with seventh chords

The chords we have seen so far consist of the first, third and fifth notes of a scale, so the next step is the seventh. A dominant seventh chord (shown simply as '7') is formed with the first, third, fifth, and flattened seventh notes of a scale. 'B' is the seventh note in the C major scale (CDEFGAB), so C7 can contain C, E, G, and B♭.

Key

1 Index **2** Middle **3** Ring **4** Little **X:** Don't strum this string

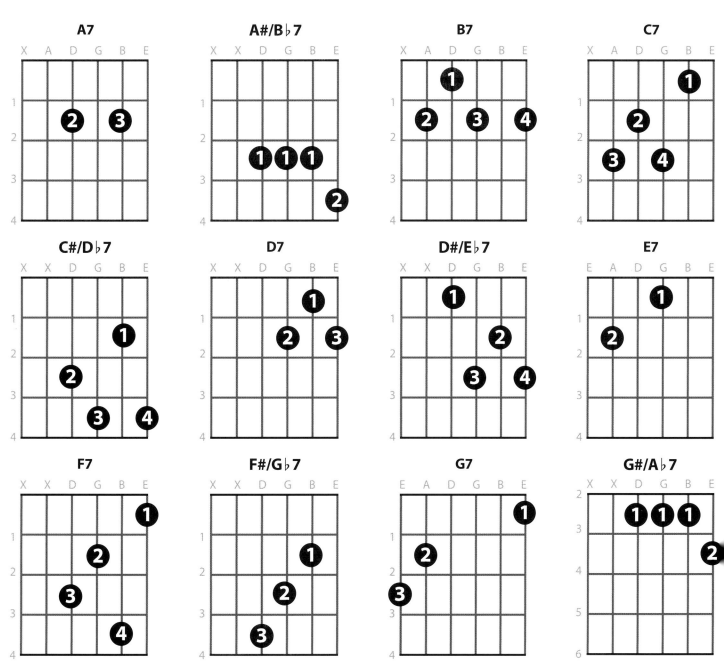

Major seventh chords

Tricky to achieve, but they're worth the effort

Major seventh chords (maj7), are similar to dominant seventh chords, but they include the natural seventh note in the major scale, rather than a flattened one. For example, Cmaj7 would feature C, E, G, and B, rather than the B♭ from the dominant, as B is the seventh note in the C major scale. Using a major seventh chord will give your tunes a warm, happy feel.

Key
❶ Index ❷ Middle ❸ Ring ❹ Little **X:** Don't strum this string

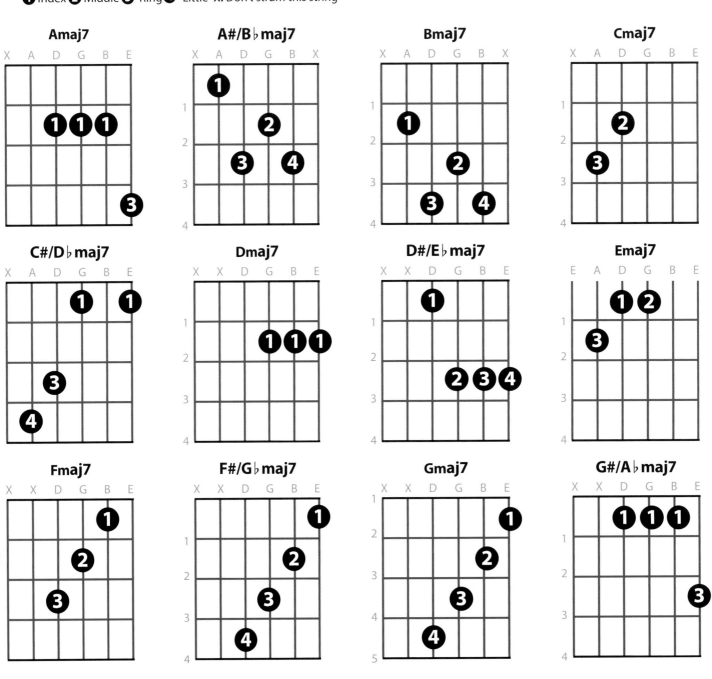

Minor seventh chords

Jazz your songs up with some m7 chords

Minor seventh chords (m7) use the flattened seventh note seen in dominant seventh chords as well as a flattened third note found in basic minor chords. So Cm7 would contain C, E♭, G, and B♭. E and B are the third and seventh notes respectively of the C major scale, and they are both flattened here to create the m7 chord.

Key

❶ Index ❷ Middle ❸ Ring ❹ Little **X:** Don't strum this string

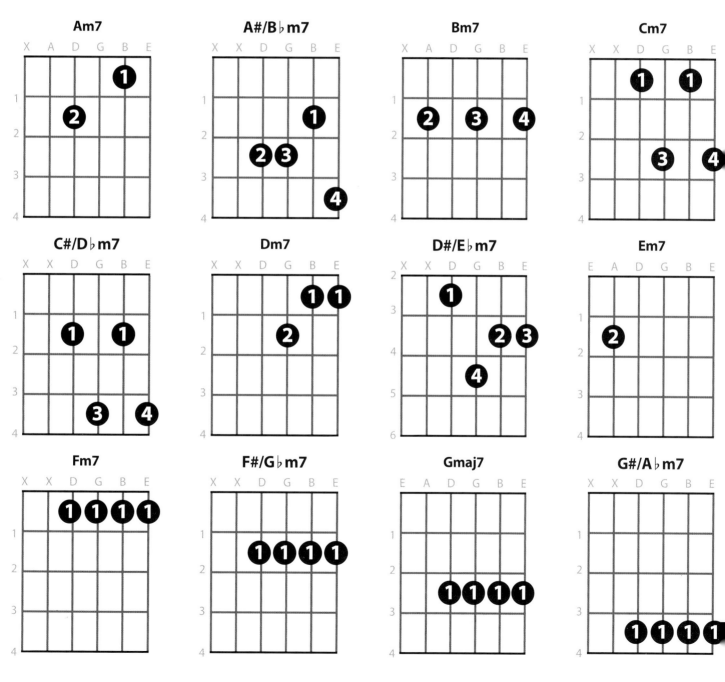

Suspended chords

Add subtle variations with suspended shapes

So far, all the chords we've looked at have featured the third note of their corresponding major or minor scale. Suspended chords (sus) don't, usually replacing it with either a second (sus2) or a fourth (sus4). So Csus4 would feature an F (the fourth note in the C major scale) instead of the E found in a major chord. Here's a list of sus4 chords.

Key

① Index **②** Middle **③** Ring **④** Little **X:** Don't strum this string

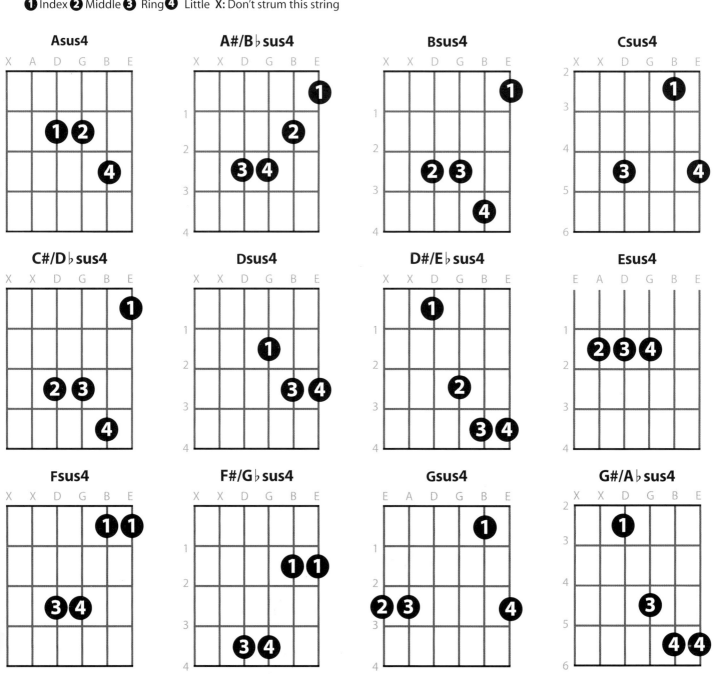

Main E-shape barre chords
Use all six strings for a rich-sounding barre chord

Here are the E-shape family of barre chords. They all come from the open E chords (E major, E minor, E7 etc) and they are probably the most popular of the barre chords, mainly because they use all six strings and therefore it's easier to strum through them, as you don't have to worry about avoiding any strings. These shapes can be used all the way up the fretboard.

Key
❶ Index ❷ Middle ❸ Ring ❹ Little **X:** Don't strum this string

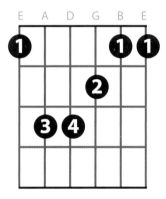

Major
The lowest note names the chord, so it is important that you know the notes on the thick E string (start at the open E and go up alphabetically with sharps/flats between all but E-F and B-C). The two thinnest strings and the thick E string are held down by the index finger, so you'll need to apply pressure at both ends.

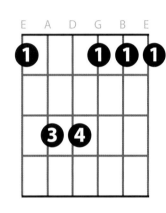

Minor
This is based on the open E-minor shape, but here the sixth, third, second and first strings are fretted by your barring index finger, so you need to apply consistent pressure. If you find yourself struggling with barre chords, this shape is the best to practise. When you've nailed it, add your middle finger and form a major shape.

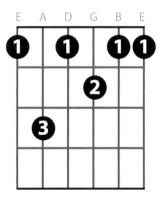

Dominant seventh
This is played like the major, only your little finger comes away from the fourth string. Make sure your barring finger is fretting the D string cleanly. This note is the flattened seventh, which gives the chord its distinct sound, so it needs to be heard. You can play an optional not on the fourth fret (when barring the first) on the B string.

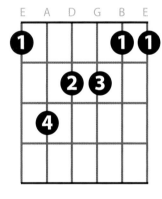

Major seventh
They're possibly the most awkward of the E-shape barre chords, but they'll sound great when you pull them off. If you're having trouble getting to grips with this shape, try using an A-shape major seventh on the next page instead. If you're doing this, barre seven frets higher than you were with the E-shape to achieve the same chord.

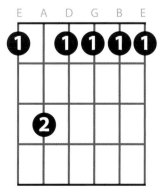

Minor seventh
It may look rather simple, with only one non-barring finger needed, but for this jazzy-sounding chord you will need to get five of the six barred strings ringing out under your index finger – no easy feat! Like the seventh, this chord contains an optional flattened seventh note that can be fretted with your little finger.

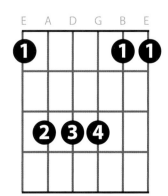

Sus4
Like the open suspended chords, suspended barre chords offer subtle variations on the familiar major sound. The shape is similar to A major, so it may feel like a tight squeeze, but soon it'll feel like second nature. It's not too tricky to transition from suspended chords, either. Just remove your little finger and you're playing a minor chord.

Main A-shape barre chords

Try out these five-string shapes

Here's the A-shape family of barre chords. They don't sound quite as full as the E-shape chords as they only use five strings, the fifth string (A) carrying the root note. So don't strum the sixth (E) string or the chord won't sound as good. Playing one of these shapes with the seventh fret barred will give you the equivalent of an open E-shape chord, just an octave higher.

Key

1 Index **2** Middle **3** Ring **4** Little **X:** Don't strum this string

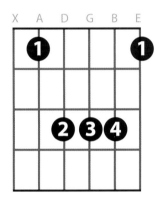

Major

This barre chord can be tricky as it is hard to get your three fretting fingers into the same increasingly narrow space in the same fret. However, you can get around this by using your index finger as the main barre and your ring finger as a mini-barre to hold down the B and G strings, leaving your little finger free.

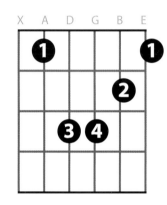

Minor

This shape can be easily moved up the neck as it is like the Emajor shape, only moved over a string. As you will notice, this chord is very similar to the A-shape major – only one note is out of alignment, which is the flattened third that makes this a minor chord. Make sure your index finger is fretting the A and thin E strings properly.

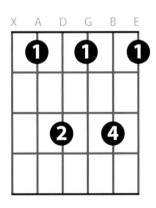

Dominant seventh

This shape is a bit more manageable than the major and it's fairly easy to transition into it – all you need to do is add your ring finger in between the two notes that you're already fretting. Try playing a dominant seventh chord, then moving five frets up the fretboard and playing a major chord for an easy progression.

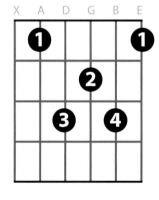

Major seventh

The 'inverted D major' shape take a bit of getting used to, but it's a much less awkward shape to play than the E-shape major seventh. Major seventh chords work well together, so try keeping the same shape in your fretting hand and play major seventh chords on the dotted frets of your guitar. You might get a jazzy little tune going!

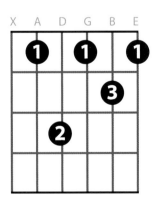

Minor seventh

This is very similar to the minor chord, but the root on the third string has been removed, allowing the barred note (the flattened seventh) to sound. As always, the root is played by the lowest note – the barred note on the A string. There is also an optional flattened seventh note that you can fret with your little finger.

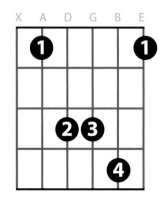

Sus4

The sus4 chord takes the A-major shape, but you fret your finger one fret higher on the B string. This is the suspended fourth, which replaces the third note normally played in a major chord. The sus2 is easier to play as you can just remove your ring finger from the fretboard entirely. Try moving from a major chord to sus4 to sus2.

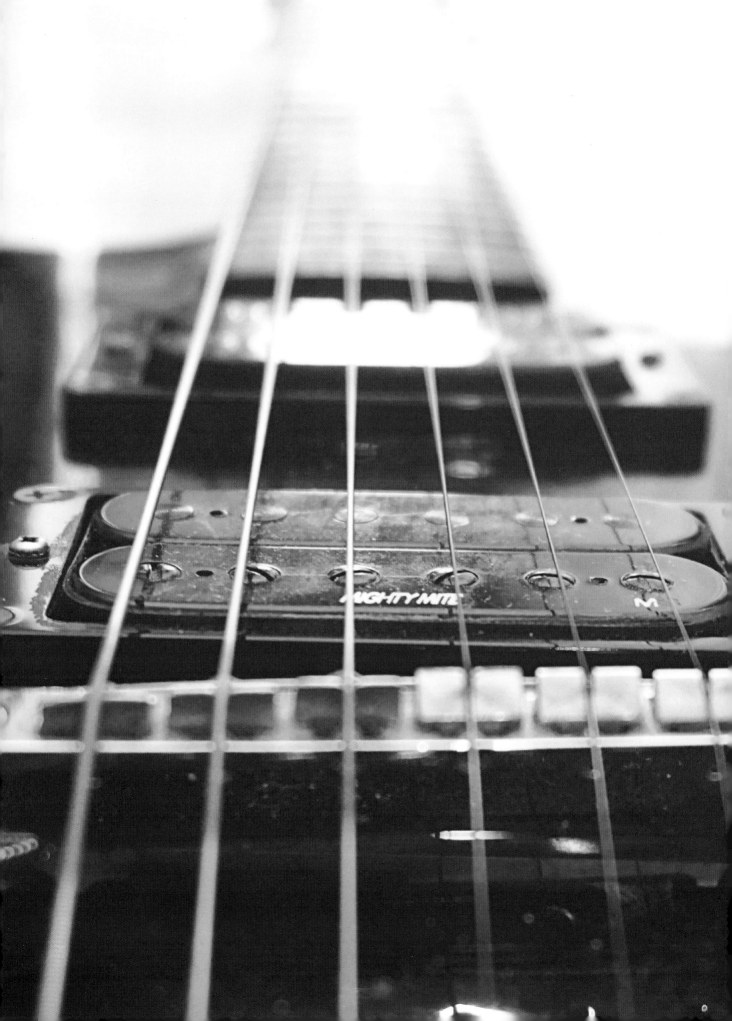

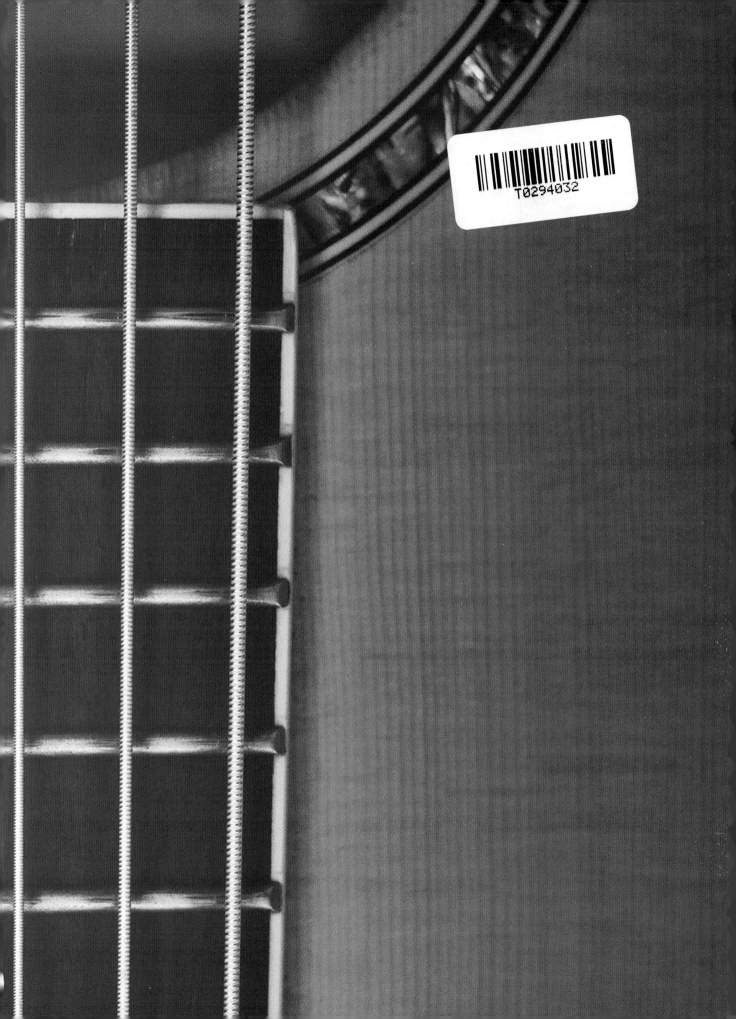